SEVEN KINGS

SEVEN KINGS

A novel by

ALAN BRAWN

set in the heart of a
London Irish
community

Published by:
savageculture
P.O. Box 1534
Ilford IG3 9FT

ISBN 0 9539646 0 4

British Library in Cataloguing in Publication Data:
a catalogue record for this book is available from the British Library.

savageculture.com

Typesetting, design & production:
Country Books, Little Longstone, Derbyshire DE45 INN

For Mark Brawn
1960 – 1982

I always flirt with death,
I look ill but I don't care
about it. Peter Perrett

CONTENTS

1. HEAD HELD HIGH

11am. Bangin' on. Every second Tuesday at the Ilford dole office.

I learned my technique from Cliff; he was the Master.

'Have you worked in the last two weeks, sir?' In a performance bettered only by Brando in *Streetcar*, Cliff gently lifted his humble head, and with the look of a soon-to-be-slaughtered Bambi, wearily delivered his immortal reply – 'Chance would be a fine thing.' This was quality Method acting, the DSS girl melted. But today we were genuinely pissed off; Eamon Mooney lined us up with a paint-job in Wapping – then, at the last minute pulled the plug, meaning the whole week was scratched.

'At least I can walk in there with me head held high today,' mused Cliff. 'Genuine unemployed, my friend!'

Genuine was a big word with us, especially with Cliff's uncle Harry; as he went round the table in the Crown – 'You're genuine; you're genuine,' looking over at Gerry behind the ramp – 'He's a tosser.' These two were usually as thick-as-thieves, but Harry had just come off a three-day ban for punching the karaoke DJ because he wouldn't let him sing 'Lady In Red' last Friday night.

Looking at me – 'You're genuine, Derry.'

'Cheers, Harry mate. Pint of Guinness?'

Thanks to a preservation order, the Crown was left virtually on its own in a derelict street, in a bustling part of East London called Seven Kings. As well as serving good beer, it was a focal point for business and social planning alike. Gerry was the landlord, a stout Irishman from Tyrone, with a penchant for giving murderous renditions of Paddy Reilly songs when he had a lock-in. Although deadly serious on the surface, Gerry was deadpan and, had a stinging sense of humour, and most of the craic in the pub revolved around him. He seemed to be aware of every conversation at each table and could join in at will – and, invariably did.

Mum was from Coalisland, Co. Tyrone, which held me in good favour with Gerry, and would allow me more slack than the other patrons, but only a bit, you couldn't take liberties with Gerry. His background was shrouded by an impenetrable shield and rumour insured that nobody overstepped the mark.

'Warmin' yer minge, Val?' Cliff was in full-flow, I never really understood the actual meaning of this, but Cliff was funny and it always forced a grin. It was one of his more pleasant greetings to a woman, and on this occasion Liz O'Grady was the lucky lady (he called all women, Val). Liz was a stunner, fit as a butcher's dog, and had been working behind the ramp since April. She was a niece of Noeleen, Gerry's wife, and was blessed with a gorgeous Donegal accent. Everyone in the pub had tried their luck, me and Cliff included. No joy.

She was a great barmaid, Liz would chat with anyone, knew all the local gossip on the various characters and villains that came into the pub, but gave little away about herself (a fine Irish trait).

'What happen' to ya face, Cliff?' asked Liz.

'I fell out the bedroom window (strangely, this wasn't unusual for Cliff) on Saturday night. Finished up in the pear tree.'

'You're not wise, boy. What the frig were yeh up to?'

'I was off me 'ead. A big squad of us went to the Glenvale and had a skinful. All I remember was tryin' to have a slash out the window.' Cliff was notorious for urinating all over his mum's maisonette when he was topped-up.

The Glenvale was an Irish-run nightclub masquerading as a traditional music venue (most of the bands they managed to attract, however, were chancers, playing middle-of-the-road 'classics') with a reputation for serving the worst pint of Guinness this side of the Blackwall Tunnel (some achievement, as competition's fierce). Cliff was often found in the Glenvale spewing his ring, bemoaning the poor condition of the Black Stuff.

Liz brought five pints of Guinness over to our table, each head expertly inscribed with a shamrock. I was joined by Kevin Devlin and Martin Sweeney, and was sucked into a deep and solemn debate regarding the Crown's much feared but useless football team. The half-serious threat by Gerry to withdraw sponsership of the kit (Blackpool-tangerine for the shirts, with milk chocolate-brown for the shorts and stockings) had introduced a ripple of anxiety to the proceedings. Gerry was citing the fact that we were tainting his pub's punctiliously built reputation.

Fair enough, we were currently banned from joining any league in the country (probably the world) affiliated to the FA, care of Kevin's brother, Rory, shooting a linesman in the neck with an airgun-dart. Our plea of 'diminished responsibility' due to Rory being an 18-carat psycho, fresh from a relaxing break in a cosy detention centre, fell on deaf ears. Four previous attacks on the officials in charge of our matches, meant the ban was decreed permanent. Martin, however, remained full of ideas and optimism – believing that a return to a basic 4-4-2 and the addition of a nippy, Pat Nevin-style winger supplying the ammo, could restore the team to the (never seen) glory days.

'You're all fuckin' pony. That's the problem!' Cliff, as usual, interrupted the soccer summit to which he was never asked to be present, because of his total lack of knowledge and interest in sporting matters.

'Derry, Eamon's on the phone; can we meet him at Kiefer's about two o'clock?' asked Cliff.

'Has he got our money?' He was into me and Cliff for seventy quid each for digging the footings for an extension round his sister-in-law's bungalow. Cliff winked – 'Yeah, he's got it. Reckons he's got some work for us, too.'

'Tell 'im three o'clock,' too late, communication was lost. Cliff's mobile had died more times than Bobby Davro.

I decided to have another crack at Liz.

'Liz, there's a small squad of us goin' down the Balls Pond Road tonight. Should be a good craic – there's a benefit dance in the Clanger. Wha' d'yeh reckon?'

'What'll the music be?' asked Liz.

'Traditional mostly. A group called Rhianna are playin'. Kev's been ravin' about 'em for ages, said they're brilliant live.'

'Sure. Why not.' My heart was pounding to the drumbeat of 'Dog Eat Dog' and a state of delirium was in close attendance. Not since Eddie Newton buried the decisive penalty at St.James' Park in a nerve-shredding shoot-out last January, had I felt this rush of adrenalin burning my intestines. I was staggered, after all, just a couple of weeks ago she'd turned down a chance to go and see Mary Black at the Royal Albert Hall.

'Who else's goin', Derry?' Liz enquired.

'Martin, Cliff, Kevin... oh yeah – Cathy Hurst and Roisin Brady, Imelda, Breda Kenna, Mick an' Davey Casey and Chris Begley – he's got the tickets.'

'Some small squad but!' beamed Liz.

'Watch that little fucker, Liz,' warned Gerry.

'Thanks for the kind reference, Gerry. She'll be safe with me. Meet yeh here at seven, Liz,' I said expectantly.

* * * * * * *

Kiefer's was empty apart from Eamon sitting at the window-table nursing a mug of tea, carefully examining the Racing Post. This was an archetypal pie'n'mash shop, ie – the food was served luke warm and the decor hadn't been touched since the early seventies.

'Two teas, Bernie.'

'Be right with yeh, Derry.' Bernie was checking over his pools coupon. 'Rita's goin' mad for gettin' this bathroom tiled, boy,' said a stressed Bernie.

'I'll ring yeh tomorrow, Bernie. These Portuguese tiles she's after are gonna cost yeh, though,' I explained.

'Bollocks to Portugese tiles,' snapped Bernie.

Eamon was seen as something of a prime-mover in the area and amongst his business interests was a strictly *un*registered loan company. He was also the owner of the pie'n'mash shop.

On and off, we'd been working for him about five years, doing all sorts, including a memorable three days 'minding girls' for his now defunct strip-a-gram agency. The debacle which led to the demise of the agency was triggered by one of the soap-dodging parasites at a students' party in Stratford, after he took a touch too much with Big Tina. The consequence of the ensuing riot that erupted, was me and Cliff being arrested and charged with affray. Although the charges were later dropped it did seem to take the shine off the project for Eamon.

'How's the form, Derry?'

'Money's tight, Eamon, you know we need to be workin'.'

'Yeah, sorry 'bout that, lads. The job was set for Monday, but youse know the score, the builders are way behind. They'll hand over next week – at the earliest.'

'Northerners, I bet, wearin' *I Built Canary Wharf* T-shirts.'

'...Is correct, Cliff. Bolton,' confirmed Eamon.

'It's okay, Eamon. What yeh got in mind now, though?' I asked.

'Right, Derry. First off; here's ya money. Youse put in a fair day, there.'

'FAIR DAY, HARRY! (Cliff always called Eamon, Harry.) We worked our nuts off round there. Me spine was 'angin' out.'

'Derry, I want you an' Cliff workin' for me full-time.'

'Cash money, Eamon?' Giving a passable, if unintentional impersonation of Bill Shankly, Eamon's response was short and sweet: 'Aye, son. Cash money.'

For Cliff, no further details were necessary, the only thought likely to flash through his brain would be 'That will do nicely, sir!' I, however, had known Eamon a long time. He was a man of imposing stature, with a physique that belied his age and, had a bright mind, which was continuously slipping through the gears, searching for the next big money-spinner.

The first time I met Eamon was at the Meadow Lane Social Club over twenty years ago. This was where the local Irish community converged on Sunday nights, and you could always tap Eamon for a bottle of Cresta.

Eamon was from Roosky, a small town in Roscommon on the border with Longford, a place I knew well from my holidays, as my dad was a Longfordman. I've spent untold hours walking alone, along the Shannonside, daydreaming, looking deep into the dark water, trying hard to understand the stark beauty of 'this Land', and to reconcile it to the reality of the overcrowded, dirty rush of London existence. Economics aside, I'm certain this is why the Irish travel the globe incessantly, to reassure themselves of their good fortune at their place of birth.

The prospect of becoming too involved with Eamon worried me; a decent bloke? Well... maybe. He was hugely entertaining drinking company – but, to be under his wing as a full-time lackey would be a dicey way to earn a crust.

My father, Patsy, worked for the Clayton Motor Company, for near on thirty years at their plant in Stepney, a magnet for Irishmen since the early fifties. Seven Kings was where they settled. The men who slaved in the deafening grind and heat of the foundry were given meagre compensation for the damage to their eardrums *and* souls. Eamon Mooney never soiled his hands working in the foundry but my dad knew well of his business.

I was staring directly at Eamon but my attention was drawn to the disturbance occuring outside. The condensation cascading down the window couldn't disguise the unruly Firm swarming past. The screaming and ballaching was punctuated only by pauses to blow smoke-rings (the rest of the smoke exiting through their noses), as they pushed past the hassled mums, whose prams were laden down with premature Christmas shopping. Decorated with earrings and West Ham United scarves, these mobsters had a mean age of eleven. School's-Out-for-EVER!

'When do we start?' Cliff asked. Wide-ranging as Cliff's skills were, a great poker player, he would not make.

'What did you 'ave in mind, Eamon?' I asked.

'I want yeh to collect for me, Derry. Loans; rent... everything. I need back-up.' Inwardly my interest began to dissolve.

True, I was in need of money (lots of it), it was common knowledge that I was in the grip of a personal recession. Three grand on one credit card, twelve hundred on another. Four thousand on a struggling Alfa Romeo and a mounting debt to my parents that was spiralling out of the control of any realistic repayment.

I'd always considered myself special, a man of real fibre and sound morals, aloof from the small-minded, selfish dregs with whom I readily mixed. But, my resolve was on the wane; a good-ish pub-player, but it was unlikely I would ever grace the San Siro; although I could sing, I wasn't going to write the 'Green Fields Of France'. The words *'Did they sound the Death March, as they lowered you down'* filtered through my conscience, as I said to Eamon: 'I won't terrorize people.' The look of feigned horror which sprang to Eamon's face was real vaudeville.

'No way, Derry, that's why I'm askin' you. This is a legitimate business proposition. No threats,' oh, silly me – 'I want yeh to be my No.1; professional; discreet.' Eamon's idea of discretion ment giving the Law a wide berth.

'Look, Derry, I've known your family a long time now; yer da's a good man. All I do is lend money to people who can't use a bank. I rent rooms to people who can't get a mortgage (I was in the presence of a latter-day Robin Hood). Most of 'em work. All I want is someone to collect, somebody I can trust.' Eamon's noble speech was cut short by the noise of the window vibrating, from severe banging by the motley looking devil outside.

Raymond was beckoning me to come out and join him. By the state of him you'd think he just crawled out from a compost heap. He was suited perfectly to his job – keeping the streets of East Ham clean.

Ray was a fish out of water. He was a Brazilian, born in a slum area of Sao Paulo; came to London to make his fortune, and ended up working for Newham Council for 21 years. As well as supporting his own family (wife and three daughters), he sent money back to Brazil each month to help feed his brother and sister's children. I made his acquaintance when a brief spell of road sweeping was added to my vast and disjointed c.v.

'*Qué-pasa?* How'd the 'oliday go, Ray?'

'Wonderful, Derry. Wonderful,' reaching into his rubbish cart, he pulled out a small packet, neatly wrapped in brown paper.

'This is for your mum, Derry. It's the coffee I promised you.'

'Nice one, Ray. I knew yeh wouldn't let me down.' Dirty as his job was, Ray enjoyed it and, had little to worry over; unlike me, where trouble was almost certainly lying in wait.

'Oi, Ray, you ol' slag. CUM'ERE!' bawled Cliff affectionately.

Cliff was also an ex-member of the Newham chain-gang and was a sometime drinking partner of Ray's. I had a lot of time for this South American scruff – he was one of a small group that asked with true sincerity about the welfare of my brother. Because of four unexplained minutes deprived of oxygen at birth, Luke came out of the delivery-room mentally handicapped.

A firm handshake seals my fate as we agree to meet Eamon at his house on Friday.

* * * * * * *

On my way to pick Luke up from his 'special' learning centre, my mind was firmly focused on Liz, more specifically, the perfect form of her arse. Turning into Beaumont Avenue, I was becoming increasingly anxious. A couple of hours was all I had to get Luke home – have some nosebag, a quick bath, get changed (purple Ben Sherman and black Levi's), before meeting up with Liz.

Difficult though it is to suppress my guilt from the lack of time I've spent with Luke recently, I convince myself he knows *and* understands why.

This was a crucial period for me, my 27th birthday was a week away and the nights on the glug with the boys were almost getting monotonous. The depression that set in from the morning after comedown (the chemical imbalance in my brain was lurching into the red zone) was becoming a far less temporary condition.

The thought of marriage and having kids actually seemed like a nice idea. Now this was really frightening, to think I may of reached the stage where this is what I want. The trappings that come with a family were never something I desired: the mortgage, the robotic tube ride or, fighting your way into the Smoke on gridlocked roads and the relentless battle against the venal scum in yellow-striped caps.

Barronmead was regarded as a flagship centre for children with Luke's disabilities, and he was as happy as a pig-in-shit. As I walked through the playground I could see Luke screaming with delight, giving Mrs Macintosh an almighty bear hug. The warmth she radiated with her smile made me feel inadequate. She was just a teacher doing her job; for many years I practically treated him like a leper.

Luke, who appeared to have zero intelligence, soaked up all my family's attention. When my mum and dad's friends came to visit, Luke was all they ever talked about – 'He's such a happy soul', I despised him, he embarrassed me – 'Your brother's a Spazey'. It's hard to admit I took so long to love him.

The specialists opinion said Luke was unlikely to communicate or even walk properly, but my parents refused to accept this. The National Health Service had discarded him as a vegetable but, Mum in particular, fought the authorities to get the best treatment possible. Luke will never know *how* hard she fought. Walking and talking were merely part of a long list of his abilities now.

'Hello, Derry,' said Mrs Macintosh.

'How are yeh, Mrs Macintosh?' I said straining, as I tried to prise Luke off her. 'Did he be'ave 'imself today?'

'He's a great lad, Derry, we don't have any trouble with Luke. The only problem's persuading him to go home!'

* * * * * * *

'Derry, Cliff said he'll be round at half-six. D'yeh want chips with this?' Carmel had all kinds of dishes frying and sizzling; baking and bubbling. My choice was steak'n'kidney pie with baby sweetcorn, peas and chips – the perfect lining for a bellyful of Guinness. Carmel always made the dinner, she was the elder of my two sisters, four years younger than me and, a blinding cook.

'There yeh go, Luke,' chicken drumsticks, chips and beans, was about the only food Luke ate voluntarily. He didn't acknowledge Carmel, shoving a drumstick straight into his mouth, with his concentration fixed solely on *The A-Team*, which was rerunning on some cable channel. Fine as the delicate puff-pastry on my pie was, I couldn't appreciate the taste to the full; the clock was ticking and, as ever, Siobhan was entrenched in the bathroom.

Siobhan was the black sheep of the family, seventeen, a regular streetwise club-goer since the age of fourteen. The rest of us in the house were more or less employed as personal assistants, to answer the phone and help arrange her social life.

'Move ya fuckin' self, Siobhan,' I growled.

'I'll be out in a minute, Derry,' came back Siobhan's usual reply.

'Fuckin' right yeh will. I've got twenty minutes to get ready.'

'DERRY! Would yeh mind watchin' that language – *please?*'

'Sorry, Ma. She's windin' me up, though. She knows I'm late.'

'Someone's at the door, Mum,' said Luke helpfully. You could gamble your Rolex on Cliff being early.

'Evening, Mrs Sheehan,' said Cliff cheerfully.

'Right, Cliff. How yeh doin', son?'

'Top-notch. Are yeh gonna come with us tonight, Mrs Sheehan, and 'ave a bit of a yee-hah!?'

'Aye, give us a second, Cliff. I'll just go an' polish up me dancin' shoes!'

'Bollocks,' a collar button fell off me Ben Sherman. Next best thing? My old faded grey Fiorucci shirt.

'Lukey, what's this shite yer watchin'?' It was Cliff who came swimming with us nearly every week for the past eight years, he probably spent as much time with Luke as I did.

'AAAAAARRRRRR...SHIT!!' Cliff and Luke rolled into the flimsy table which was home for a spread of manky plant-life, causing mass devastation. Panicking, Luke shot in immediately with his defence: 'That's Cliff's fault, Mum, he was bending me arm back.'

'Jesus, Cliff, could yeh not be more careful? Those plants die of thirst in this house as it is,' said Mum attacking Cliff. Luke was beaming, sniggering quietly Muttley-style.

A liberal dousing of *Obsession For Men* and we're ready for battle.

'Okay, Ma, we're off now. See-yeh later.'

'Right, Derry,' giving Cliff the eagle eye. 'Try an' take it easy, lads. Derry, don't forget you're takin' me and yer da over to Geraldine's in the mornin',' said Mum looking troubled.

'Don't worry, Mrs Sheehan, we're not goin' on a session. It's the music we're after – maybe a couple of pints,' Mum's eyebrows gave the only response.

* * * * * * *

The Crown was five minutes walk from our house in Burnley Road; three, if you cut through St. Mary Magdalan churchyard and slipped down the Valley Parade alleyway. It left you spitting distance from the saloon-bar entrance of the Crown. As we reached the top of the alley, Paddy Meegan spun in – swaying, and obliterated by drink.

'Derry... boy. How's it... goin', son?' spluttered Paddy.

'Sweet as a nut, Paddy. Are yeh winnin'?'

'Ah.. fuck, Derry – I'm gone.'

'Sniffin' the barmaid's apron again, Paddy?' asked Cliff.

'Rejoice in the Lord, Cliff. Always again I sing rejoice.'

'Fare enough,' Cliff nodded in agreement.

'Are yeh comin' down the club on Friday, Paddy, they've got the Line dancin' mob in again? Should be a giggle.'

'I'll never show me face, Derry. I t'ink I'm barred; as regards Brendan... yeh know – he's a prick.'

'Bren's alright. I'll see-yeh down there, Paddy.'

'That's it, Derry. Dead on,' slurred Paddy as he staggered off.

Pushing open the door, my stomach was beginning to

churn, as my thoughts skipped uncontrollably forward in the progress I was hopefully going to make with Liz. God, she was tasty – not flash. Shoulder length black hair, dazzling clear blue eyes that left me helplessly exposed and, great skin; she *was* CLASS.

'Oh, Jimmy, will yeh piss-off, will yeh?' said Liz to Jimmy Duffy, who'd been ogling her and salivating at the bar.

'Sorry about that, Derry. Your Guinness is on, *darrlin'*.'

'DARLIN'... DARLIN'!! Bloody 'ell, it's not what yeh know in this fuckin' pub,' cried Cliff.

'Don't yeh just luv it, Cliff!? I'll be with youse in a sec, Derry. I'm just givin' Noeleen a hand till the rush dies.'

'We're okay for time, Liz. The band won't be on 'til eleven.'

* * * * * * *

Surprisingly, the tingling sensation electrifying my spine was not induced by my right thigh nestling with a slight tremble up against Liz's thigh. Desperate though I was to discover a sexual chemistry, this joyous feeling was brought on by five pints of Guinness and the wonderous intro to 'Love Will Tear Us Apart', as the thumping drums and jangly guitars came crashing out from the jukebox.

It was still a good hour before the band were to come on and I'd given up trying to be funny and interesting. Stringing a half-coherent sentence together was the best I could aspire to. I decide to take Noel Gallagher's wise advice – *'You need to be yourself. You can't be no-one else'*.

Despite my rapidly deteriorating condition, things were going pretty well. Plenty of sustained eye contact, no uncomfortable silences – Liz was even keen to meet the rest of the clan. Martin came zigzagging across the floor with a precariously balanced tray of Guinness and Pernod – and, just managed to touchdown and avert an elephantine disaster. Liz and Roisin were immersed in a fiercely animated exchange concerning the girl in a microskirt who had attached herself to Chris, and was now bent over the pool table revealing her even more minuscule panties, as she took position for her next shot.

'That blade's a friggin' menace. She was after sellin' Es in the Glen last Saturday,' said Roisin.

'Aye, she's givin' a fair show for the boys. I've not seen her before. Where's she from?' asked Liz.

'Manor Park. She's an ol' bike.' Roisin was from Keady, Co. Armagh, and was working at the London Hospital as an auxiliary nurse. She was a scream, lethal company, and would mesmerize you with her humour and charm when recounting sordid tales from the wards involving *doctors and nurses*.

The only action that could save me when I was starting to sag through drink was a great song. And so, as Martin reached the jukebox, with eager voices shelling him with suggestions from all directions, he gave us 'The Bottle' – '*See that black boy runnin' wild, over there, his ol' man's got a problem,*' my lungs close to collapsing, as I let rip: 'NA-NA-NA-NA AND A BOTTLE O' WINE.'

Feeling suitably refreshed, we targeted Chris, who sat down to a torrent of abuse and derision, as he waited for Micro to emerge from the bog – 'Are yeh fuckin' desperate, Chris?'

'Och, leave 'im alone, Roisin, he's not doin' any harm but. God fuckin' luv 'im like,' pleaded Liz.

Cliff was less charitable: 'What yeh done with Scabbie Maggie? Is she still doin' the modellin' for Pedigree Chum?'

'She's prob'ly doin' a line in the khazi,' offered Davey.

'Wanker, Casey. At least she doesn't rattle like Pipa.'

'Calm down, Chris. Davey's been with ev'ry reptile in Barking,' I announced informatively.

''Ark at 'im, Squiddly Diddly. I'd be careful with him, Liz, when he dives off the wardrobe in his Batman gear,' roared Davey.

'Yeah, tryin' to do butterfly in his water bed. Make sure yeh bring your rubber ring, Liz,' added Cliff. Although too pissed to be embarrassed, I was nevertheless grateful the band appeared.

'HOW YEH DOIN', PEOPLE? It must be three years since we were last here, it's great to see youse out in force tonight,' and then? Straight into a blistering cover of 'N17'.The Clanger was chocka, as packed as I'd ever seen it. Benefit nights always engendered a special buzz.

Glancing across at Liz I was pleased to find her eyes burning into mine, and, with a broad smile on her face, clearly she wasn't bothered about the state I was in. Liz clasped her hand round the back of my neck, the relief was immeasurable; CONTACT!

'Jes', you're right, Derry, this band are pure class.' A funny thing alcohol and perfume, for at this precise moment, the smell of Liz was breathtaking.

Martin and Cliff had paired up with some girls from Dublin and were going through their well drilled and perfectly delivered chat. Chris and Micro were spinning out of control beneath the speakers displaying an almost painful lack of rhythm.

'STACKS OF CLARET!' bellowed Cliff, accompanied with a hand signal (left hand held two inches from mouth, fingers stretched stiff and upwards). This was my cue to replenish the liquor and reluctantly I peeled away from Liz, accidentally brushing her breasts with my chest as I went by.

Cliff had switched on to autopilot with his new friends, the interchange with Martin so slick, unsuspecting bystanders could be forgiven for believing the Marx Brothers had been reincarnated and planted *Terminator*-like in the public bar of the Clanger. I tried to put myself in the place of these milky-skinned beauties, back to the first time I'd heard and, contributed, to the threadbare material.

I was continually astounded by the enthusiasm Cliff was able to summon when regurgitating these over-used lines. Were they still amusing? Probably not, 'it's the way yeh tell'em', though. One thing I was sure about; the Guinness had become sterile in taste. Moving from hand to mouth in a mechanical motion, I was drinking on pride and instinct alone as the black liquid swirled down my gullet. The unthinkable had to be considered: miss myself out of the next round, *ooooh*!

Eventually I wriggled to within striking distance of the bar. I was met by the unmistakable whine of Dent Head Derek, so-named, after taking the mother of all beatings outside the Ilford Palais when he was a mere pup.

'Alright, Derry mate, what yeh doin' 'ere?' I'd heard Del was trying to climb the ladder and move from user to pusher, which he promptly confirmed.

'Listen, Derry, I've got some quality Charlie, very clean.'

'Forget it, Del. I'm not into powder.'

'Cliff'll take some. Where is 'e?'

'Look, Del; fuck-off. We're not buyin'.' Sod-it, I'll try one more pint; I'm *'young an' good-lookin' '* etc.

'Grab that, Cliff,' I said juggling with the drinks.

'Derry, cum 'ere an' meet Lauren and Dervilia,' said Cliff.

'How youse doin', have yeh managed to hear the band yet with this pair bustin' yer balls?'

'Well... not much!' said a slightly hesitant Dervilia.

'They're 'avin' the time of their lives with us two. What more could they want!?' bragged Cliff.

'Bring Liz over, Derry,' said Martin.

'We'll be over, mate. Let me get rid of these drinks first.'

Making my way back to Liz, the stage smoke began to clear, and I caught sight of her mouthing the words to 'Deportees'. She was into the music; great. Besides this welcome discovery, when seen in profile, and captured in a certain light (dark), Liz was a dead-spit for Ellen Barkin (ecstasy). A first tentative swig of Guinness slid down my throat... no problem: I'M BACK!

The band finished their set at 1am, the resident DJ taking the reins till 3am. Opening record? Al Green – 'Let's Stay Together', and, here starteth part-one of the 'erection section'.

'Dance, Derry?' asked Liz.

'You askin'?' I replied.

'Up Yours!' These words will remain etched in my memory: first date – first smooch – WOW! There's nothing to compare with the first 'slowie' with the girl who's been the object of your most wild and vivid dreams for the past six months. Unfortunately this moment of sublime pleasure was destroyed. Shuffling round 180°, I clocked Cliff; from there on in, I could think only of his ears as I drifted back to Kiefer's and his behaviour there today. He spent the entire afternoon jabbing into his ears with a cocktail stick in an effort to loosen the crud inside. This was his way of preparing for his annual visit to the E.N.T clinic to have his ears syringed. He'd been bugging me all day about his fuckin' ears. I could hear his voice firing cannonballs across the vowels of Bryan Ferry, drowning out 'Avalon' with his graphic description to Dervilia of his imminent operation to have his brains sucked out through his ears.

Chris was practically leaving imprints on Micro's arse, and the desire to do likewise with Liz was powerful but, waltzing around to Lionel *'Hello, is it me you're looking for?'* Richie, was just not gonna happen. Thankfully I'd got my second wind, that state you sometimes mysteriously reach when the alcohol cancels itself out. Reviving, I felt a welcome familiarity with Liz, the fluid conversation seldom dipped.

'I was wonderin', Derry, I think I've met your Carmel. Does she work in Finnegan's?'

'She does, been there since she left school.'

'Aye, I booked me ma's flight there. She's lovely-lookin' but.'

'Jesus, don't tell her that!'

'Ah c'mon, she's a rare girl now.'

'You don't 'ave to live with her.'

'She seems very nice.'

'Well, yeah, compared to Siobhan,' I conceded.

'She was in the Crown last Friday – big squad. Maria Culkin an' that crowd.'

'Celebratin' her birthday. They went to see The Levellers after at the Brixton Academy. Soapy bastards.'

'I think they're great, Derry; very melodic.'

'Hippies. When you've seen The Clash play 'Spanish Bombs' at the Lyceum Ballroom – clowns like them don't qualify,' I said smugly.

'The Clash – what's that?' asked Liz innocently.

'WHAT!? You kids!'

Midway through Marvin's 'Sexual Healing', Chris ushered Micro off the dance floor and away out the door.

'Some blade, Derry!' observed Liz.

'Chris'll sort her out. He's a madman... Totally wired.'

'How 'bout wee Luke, Derry, is he doin' well?'

'He's not so wee, Liz. He's doin' great – make his day meeting you.'

'Honestly, Derry, I'd love that.'

The last dance ('Cry Me A River'), Martin and Cliff were sorted. Cliff being the sentimental type, though, insisted we all retire to the Casbah; unadulterated dog meat in a pitta. Only the white heat of the chilli sauce could numb the taste of this garbage.

Cliff was revving up again – 'Fifteen tried an' fifteen died at the hands of Mario's chilli,' no pause for breath. 'Cum on, Val, get it down ya neck.' He was flying, he must of bumped into Del. 'I saw a mouse. WHERE? *There* on the stairs.' Coke? Speed? Both!? 'A little mouse with clogs on,' mercifully braking off – 'Derry, we'll get a cab back to mine. There's three cases of Stella and a bottle o' rum left,' the remnants of the latest French foray.

'I'll swerve, mate. The Guinness in the Clanger's paralysed me. Barrel was rotten,' I said feebly.

'You're turnin' into a fuckin' tart, that's all,' said Cliff shamed by my excuse.

Imelda and Roisin had long since defected to a rave in Hoxton. The rest of us piled into a Nissan Prairie, with me in the front keeping the Nigerian mini-cab driver stimulated with my probing questions – 'What time d'yeh start, mate? What time d'yeh finish? These Nissans, reliable are they?' My quest for information was futile, each enquiry was met with the same Miss World smile and glazed eyes. No matter, he didn't try to rip us off; sixteen quid for six raucous juiceheads.

I got out at the Crown with Liz, Martin and Lauren were tongue-to-tongue, oblivious of the world around them. The rubbernecked driver looked perturbed; it brought to mind the

'No Petting' sign at the swimming-pool.

'I'll phone yeh in the mornin', Derry.'

'Not too early, Cliff,' I said with forlorn hope.

The bitter chill cut through me, my cheeks red and numb; I was sober now. The silence was broken by the rumbling of a milk float as it chugged past. Amazingly I once considered this as a career option: early start – early finish, darting about the streets of a dead metropolis while everyone dreamt, then, back in time for *Richard and Judy*. The romance of it all – The Loneliness Of A Medium Distance Milkman. Be'ave! Like all jobs, the gravy train was derailed. Now, you had to be self-employed and buy the milk off the dairies, and the wages were pitiable. As Ernie 'sped' off into the horizon, I wondered what possible motivation could force the poor sap to desert his pit at three o'clock in the morning.

'Will yeh come in, Derry, I'll make us a holy cuppa tey?'

'I don't wanna give Gerry an excuse to slag me. He'll prob'ly come chargin' down with both barrels smokin'.'

'Aye... well, he's not just that bad, Derry.'

'You could make me some tea in the bar tomorrow, Liz.'

'Mmmm... *that* I'd pay to see!' she's too sweet... too nice.

'Goodnigh', Derry.'

'Nite, Liz,' no kiss.

* * * * * * *

'Well, Derry,' aunt Geraldine's house, as always, was organized bedlam. Seven kids fighting to claim their space; from two-year-old Daragh up to Kathleen, who was nudging eighteen. The kitchen and bathroom were the primary battlefields, but today's action was taking place in the concrete yard next to the back garden. A big squad led by Seán (Geraldine's fourth-in-line) had assembled and, although only ten, and some three years the junior of most of the other recruits on parade, he was the head of the posse that conspired to 'round up', not one, but two hedgehogs.

Despite the overcrowding and headaches that arise from so many vibrant personalities crammed into a three-bed semi, this was a heart-warming place to visit. Geraldine was a remarkable woman, even after the wear'n'tear suffered giving life to seven angelic children, she still kept a super-slim figure, coupled with an inexhaustible stock of energy and caustic comments for the wee'uns.

'Mornin', Geraldine,' I croaked.

'Did we overdo it, Derry?' asked Geraldine.

'Perish the thought.' Geraldine dragged the coffee table across the carpet in readiness for our tea and buns.

'He wants to get himself a proper job. He's keepin' the hours of a friggin' vampire,' the old man glided effortlessly into his favourite hobby; ballaching me to get a 9-5.

'Let 'im alone, Patsy. He's got an interview on Friday for a full-time job. That right, Derry?' said Mum loyally.

'Yeah, I've been headhunted by a big corporation,' I crowed.

'That's right, Kentucky Fried Chicken are lookin' for a new chief spice mixer – our Derry's made the shortlist!' sniggered Dad.

'Very droll, Papa. You're a real comedian: watch him choke when I pull up in a P-reg Saab convertible.'

'Oh Jesus now, I'm holdin' me breath!'

'That's enough, Pat,' said Mum.

'MUUUUUM... QUICK!!' yelled Sheila gasping for air as she came pegging in like a bat out of hell.

Sheila was another one of Geraldine's brood, and was

prone to hysteria. Geraldine put a steadying hand on her shoulder.

'Right, pet. What's up now?'

'One of the hedgehog's fell on to its back. I think he's dead.'

'CHHRRIST! Could yeh believe this house?' Geraldine's normally tranquil weekday-morning was cruelly shattered. The prayers of the local delinquents were answered when the heating system at St.Joseph's School was poleaxed; the flooding of the headmaster's office and the science labs providing most merriment.

Looking out from the kitchen window pandemonium was rife, with thirty or more kids ducking and diving, circling the scene like ravenous vultures. The exasperated frown on Geraldine's face was not an uncommon sight.

'Shall I send for Rolf Harris?' I suggested.

'Yeh know where yeh can stick *him!* Seán's after feedin' the hedgehogs cream soda an' Coco Pops – *mixed!*'

'Ah... a priest, then,' I decided.

With one eye trained like a Rapier missile on the shenanigans going on outside, Geraldine poured the tea. Seán was giving the thumbs up, indication of a miraculous recovery by the spiked one.

'This job, Derry. What's it about?'

'Financial really – supply an' demand. The retrieval of monies from one source to a secondary base,' I said bullshitting.

'What the hell are yeh talkin' about, Derry?' asked a bemused Geraldine.

'Collectin' for Eamon Mooney.'

'Ya jokin' me, Derry?'

'It's only a trial. I might not take it, anyway.'

'C'mon, Derry. You're worth more than that, son.'

Geraldine's reaction was no surprise, but it was a sure sign of the flak that would follow.

'Yeh'll have fun sellin' this to Patsy.'

'I'll see what happens Friday, it's no big deal.'

'Good luck to yeh, son. You're gonna need it!'

Seán twisted his head round the patio-door, flashing a sideways glance at Geraldine, before snatching an iced bun from the plate of cakes and fancies destined for the front-room.

'Oi, scram. Away with yeh, Seán,' neatly stooping to avoid the dish cloth propelled towards his head, Seán set about signing me up for the footie team.

'Derry, are yeh comin' out for a kick-around, we're organizing a match?'

'Twenty-a-side again?'

'Nah, 17 versus 15.'

'Why not 16 each?'

'Danny Flint's leg's in plaster.'

'Which one?'

'His right.'

'He's right-footed, Seán. What we gonna do – drag him up to the penalty box and lift him on me shoulders to nod in the corners?'

'He's playing in goal, he can still dive. He's like Spiderman, I swear.'

'Have yeh got a proper ball yet?'

'Yeah, Bugsy's got a leather'un.'

'Good. I'll be out when I've finished me tea.'

'Okay, Derry, we're Brazil.'

'What's wrong with Ireland?'

'They're crap since Jack left.'

'Too true. I'll be Ronaldo.'

'I'm Ronaldo, I bagsy'd it already.'

'I'll be Derry Sheehan, then.

'But you're shit, Derry,' said Seán without a trace of a smile.

'SEÁN! You just apologize to Derry, that's disgustin' language to be usin' now,' commanded Geraldine.

'I was only jokin', Mum. Sorry, Derry,' said a repentant Seán.

'That lad's terror altogethe',' sighed a weary Geraldine.

'When I walk on that pitch, Seán – *you're dead,*' I promised.

The pitch in question, was the concrete yard, littered with an assortment of obstacles, including two burnt-out cars (Datsun Cherry and a Yugo). Daragh was bouncing from one end of the yard to the other, like a deranged Zebedee, on his over-inflated Space Hopper. This had been passed down the ranks and was now badly scuffed; the original bright yellow colour just a fading memory.

The game was brought to an abrupt halt when Daragh was removed unceremoniously from his rubber friend and launched into orbit by a miss-hit cross/shot. By no means a wimp, Daragh's distress was due entirely to the hopper zooming in the opposite direction to himself and it disappearing down the slope which led to the main road. Seán set off in hot pursuit, closely followed by Bugsy's one-eared mongrel, Tuna, in a vain attempt to intercept it before meeting the traffic and instant deflation.

In my unofficial capacity as a peace envoy with FIFA, my diplomatic skills were urgently required to stem the flow of bad blood circulating through the team. Tom Corney and Michael Sands were talking murder.

'What's the point me being in the box when you don't look, let alone pass?' asked a disgruntled Tom.

'Why should I pass to you? Every time you get it, you shit ya pants and fall over,' countered Michael.

Tom unleashed a bruising right-hook, sending Michael reeling backwards. Players from both sides directed an enthusiastic chant of *Dead Man Walking* at Tom, as Michael rose to his feet and dispatched a thunderous rabbit punch, which saw Tom stagger, and finally crumple to a heap on the ground.

'I was only messin' about, yeh didn't 'ave to go mental,' said Tom blubbing.

'That's what happens when you play with the big boys. Just call me Iron Mike!' Michael was strutting about the pitch, flexing his undeveloped muscles.

'Now now, girls, let's not get bitchy,' I said trying to bring a semblance of order.

'He's a big poof, Derry. Don't worry about 'im.'

'I do worry about him, Michael, because he'll be tellin' his mummy that I was standin' there watchin' while you spanked him senseless, and, quite rightly, she'll want to know why I didn't stop yeh – COMPREHENDO!!?'

'Sorry, Derry. What am I supposed to do, though? He can't trap the ball; he can't pass the ball; he can't head the ball... he's useless,' argued Michael.

'All I know, Michael, is this – if I ever manage to get you lot into a proper league; you goin' round maimin' your own team-mates is gonna leave us with a definite disadvantage when it comes to winnin' matches.'

'You punched Millbank's manager last year in the County Final.'

'That was different, I was unacceptably provoked. The maniac threw a quarter-piece of orange at me head as I was surgin' down the wing,' I said as justification for my aggression.

'Yeah, but you called him a muvver's cu—' I interrupted.

'Alright alright, yeh know what I mean. A bit of discipline's all I want. Anyway, it's not *do as I do*, it's *do as I say*.'

'I'll be'ave like Gary Lineker next season, I promise.'

'Don't go over-the-top, Michael.'

I tried to get the game re-started: 'Right, first team to reach thirty can 'ave a can of Coke each.'

Brian Sullivan was pawing at a gash on his shin, smearing the dribbling blood over his conveniently coloured (crimson) Le Shark Sportif T-shirt.

'Derry, I think I need stitches, the blood's runnin' out of me. I think I'm gonna faint,' squawked Brian.

'Shut up, Brian. If yeh wanna play for my team, you've got to take the knocks like a man. Go an' see Geraldine, she'll give you a bun an' some squash,' I said sympathetically.

After a sudden attack of apathy, the match was abandoned.

Final score: Brazil 27 Ireland 19

2. SOCIAL POLICY

Eamon's residence was located in the 'Bel-Air' of Seven Kings, on the highly coveted bungalow estate; home to the rich and famous(ish). The roll-call of 'made' men, was headed by two veterans of *Grange Hill* and a crestfallen link-man who once graced L!VE TV. Cliff was lost in the grandness surrounding us.

'Derry, look at that knob'ead, there. Nineteen, if that, and the bastard's drivin' a fuckin' TVR!'

'College boy. Daddy bought it,' I said venomously.

'That car's worth more than me ol' girl's poxy maisonette.'

I tried (and failed) to dampen Cliff's dream of a gold rush: 'Listen, mate, we'll take it one step at a time, easy yeah. A couple of days trial. If he gives us any bollocks, we quit.'

'I know I know, I'm not thick. But look at this place, Derry, it's a fuckin' palace,' said Cliff excitedly.

I parked in Eamon's drive, next to his mint-green Jaguar. Cliff was right, Eamon's drum did have a certain palatial, even stately appearance. I managed to jam the musical doorbell, detonating an eardrum-perforating high-pitched squeal that was a second cousin twice removed to 'Amazing Grace'. The oak door was flung open with violent intent, revealing Nancy, Eamon's 'glam' wife. Clearly, she was not elated with our presence.

'Sorry, Nancy. Nice tune,' I said sheepishly.

A born-again snob, she was even attempting to convince Eamon to take elocution lessons, insisting it would enhance his business and improve his chances with the Masons. Nancy was a native of Tottenham, her mum and dad had a stall in

Walthamstow Market for years, selling underwear, but Nancy's ambition was to join the Pimm's and Pony set of Emerson Park. She was seldom seen adorning Eamon's arm at the club, even going AWOL on St. Patrick's night. This was the cause of great embarrassment for Eamon, as he was now a Big Man down there, care of his new found status as Chairman of the Golf Society.

'Are yer mum'n'dad still flogging the undies, Nance?' If looks could kill, Cliff would be sleeping with the fishes. Nancy held a passionate hatred for Cliff.

'No. They're retired. What's it got to do with you anyway?'

'Blast. I was lookin' for somethin' special for me new bird.'

'Try Oxfam,' said a stern faced Nancy, with sarcasm rather than humour.

'They're too trendy now!' Cliff gave a devilish smile as Nancy marched us through to the lounge.

'You've visitors, Eamon.' Sprawled out, and luxuriating in the comfort of his recliner, Eamon was the picture of contentment.

The lurid pink-leather suite dominated in the bland, battleship-grey back-room. Three evenly spaced out photos hung on the wall above the telly. Pope John Paul II and JFK were accompanied, somewhat bizarrely, by a grinning Eddie Large (Eamon's partner in a 'showbiz' golf tournament). Needless to say, the latter was his pride and joy: 'Great comic; lovely touch with the sand wedge.'

'Ah... boys. Youse caught me nappin'. Nancy, could yeh bring us some tea, luv, and a plate of the lemon slices,' Eamon curled his lips to signify his love of the aforesaid cake.

'Are yeh still frettin' about the job, Derry?' asked Eamon.

'No. I just want things straight in me head.'

'You'll be takin' a weight off me, Derry. I mean that, now.

I'm gettin' too old to be out knockin' on doors all day. I need time to plan – you're goin' to be my right-hand man; No.1.'

'Yeah, you said,' I reminded him less than enthusiastically.

'What number will I be?' Cliff's enquiry secured a contemptuous glare from Eamon.

Eamon's recliner catapulted back into the upright position, and sent Nancy's little baby, Busker (a Persian cat), scuttling for sanctuary.

'Damn thing's a bloody death trap.' Eamon eased his way over to his desk with both hands supporting his back. After a long drawn out yawn, he unlocked the bottom drawer, pulling out a bundle of rent books.

'The rent's the bread an' butter, Derry. You'll find they're decent, good payers.' Eamon dumped the rent books into my lap.

'There's a few stragglers, mind, who'll need a bit of coaxing.'

'How many's a few?' asked Cliff suspiciously.

'Cliff, I've great confidence in your powers of persuasion, son. You're my secret weapon.'

'How many dollars?' Cliff cut to the chase.

'Four hundred pounds... netto!'

'That's a lot of confidence,' Cliff's eyes met with Nancy's as she arrived with the refreshments. Eamon lifted a lemon slice, wolfing it down in one hit before Nancy had a chance to set the tray down on the table. To her evident annoyance, Eamon's second slice left crumbs strewn all over the carpet.

'This is very civilized, Eamon.'

'It's the only way to conduct business, Derry,' Eamon raised his tea cup: 'To a prosperous future; *sláinte!*'

'*Sláinte!*' echoed Cliff.

'*Sláinte!*' I was happy. Nancy didn't join the toast, choosing instead to roll her eyes to the sky fruit machine fashion.

'Youse can start with Ruby Kavanagh,' this wiped the smile off my face good style.

'Wonderful.' Ruby had run the sweet shop in Green Street for donkey's years, and was, without exception, the most thoroughly miserable article it had been my misfortune to cross swords with.

'How much does she pay?' I asked.

'£90 a week, that's cheap, too. It's been the same for five years now. We'll be liftin' it up £30 this month, you'll need to let her know.'

'£30 a month?'

'£30 a week,' was Eamon's answer.

'You've gotta be kiddin', she'll 'ave a seizure.'

'Sure, I could get double, I'm doin' the old cow a favour.'

'Does it include the flat above?' asked Cliff.

'It does surely. I could double me money with the council, get a single mum an' her brats in.'

Eamon's empire was run without any feeling of guilt, business was booming; the Tory government positively championed the likes of Eamon. The decline in the local authorities' building programme was aiding and abetting the growth of the private landlord, the statistics (in this case) tell all: 185,000 council houses were built in Britain in 1969, in 1995 they built less than 3,000. Add to this the sale of over a million council houses since 1980, and, their shambolic housing policy was complete. Was there really a problem with living in a house, paying rent till you croak, then, a new family (or yours) moving in? Apparently we need to own the space we live in, it makes us better off, 'a man of property' and, when you're too old to empty a pint or get your leg over, it's ready to pass on to the kids. They'll flog it and divvy up the proceeds before the dust has settled on your coffin.

Eamon slid open the patio doors: 'Come an' get some air, lads. Look what the bastard vandals have done to me poor fish pond.' As if having three of his gnomes (baptized Brady, Stapleton and O'Leary) decapitated wasn't crime enough to cope with, the dirty scoundrels maximized the trauma by nicking his prize-winning Koi carp.

'This wouldn't happen in Ireland, Derry. Never.'

'You should move back, Eamon. London's goin' down the toilet, and it'll get worse. Surely you can afford to go?'

'It's not that simple. Nancy would never leave. They don't have as many shops there for her to waste me money in.'

'Shame,' I said supportively.

'What about yourself, Derry?'

'It's my destiny, mate. Given half a chance, I'll return.'

'Aye, yeh was only a wee ba, Derry.'

'Yeah, two. Biggest mistake the ol' man ever made.' Although they were married in London, Mum and Dad returned to Ireland and lived in the North for two years. Dad was happy in Tyrone, but work and money were in short supply, so the Belfast ferry brought us to England.

'Garden's lookin' well, Eamon... *a little paradise.*'

'It's a retreat from the pollution outside, Derry. Here, have a smoke.' Eamon handed me a roll-up – leaving it for me to lick the paper: 'Thanks, just what I needed to clear me lungs!' I coughed.

'Cliff?' Eamon invited him to join us.

'No, mate. My body's a temple, besides, I only smoke spliffs!'

'You'll need to chase Jimmy Wild tomorrow, too.'

'Jimmy the Ferret... where's he residin'?'

'The Prussia.' Jimmy was a maverick Limerick man, and his

slide into alcoholism curtailed what could now of been a lucrative way of making a living teaching Irish dancing (who would of predicted a few years back – the rich pickings to be claimed worldwide from entering the superkingdom that is, RIVERDANCE!?).

'Did he take a loan?' I asked knowing full well the answer.

'Five hundred in March; went home for his ma's funeral.'

'How's he payin' it back?'

'Hundred a month – plus interest,' said Eamon frowning.

'Is he keepin' up?'

'NO,' said Eamon emphatically.

'He was a world-champion dancer in his day, Eamon. Jimmy should be famous now – he was always a decent sort.'

'He's a desperate character, Derry; yeh can't put in what God left out,' said Eamon tossing his dog-end into the runner beans.

'I'll have to be slingin' youse out, fellas – we're away for a feed in town.'

'Chinese?' asked Cliff.

'Cantonese,' replied Eamon.

'My favourite. Will you ask Nancy to get me a doggy-bag?'

Eamon gave me a full-list of names, dates and amounts to be paid. His network of clients was more extensive than I imagined. Quickly scanning the list, I checked to see if there was anyone that I, or my parents knew. So far so good – maybe I could get away with this job after all.

****

Saturday morning, December 1st... I picked Cliff up at 7am. We agreed it was best to tackle Ruby early-doors; try an catch her off-guard. We were both in a buoyant mood: Cliff because

Eamon had given him a week's wages in advance – and me, because Liz said 'why not' to a quiet drink down the club after her evening shift at the Crown.

Ruby and I went back a long way; she shopped me eighteen years ago for nicking a single Bazooka Joe bubble-gum. Phoned my school and everything – even called the police. She reminded me of Olive from *On The Buses* – only less attractive.

Ruby dipped her head – her eyes peering over the glasses which balanced on her bulbous nose. I tried to break the ice, saying the first thing to enter my head: 'That Turkish Delight stuff – does anybody actually buy it, Rube?'

'Not many. They don't know what sweets are,' she said staring at me, seemingly awaiting an answer.

'Er... no!' I said puzzled, as I searched for an informed reply.

'Buttered Brazils. I bet yeh don't know what Buttered Brazils are, do yeh?' challenged Ruby.

'Course I do. They used to sell 'em in the tuck shop in Priory Road.' This revelation didn't exactly knock her bandy.

'Mars bars... bloody Mars bars, that's all they want to talk about these days,' Ruby's face was getting glummer by the second.

'Philistines, Ruby. You're serving philistines,' said Cliff.

'Phyllis who?' wondered Ruby.

'Listen, Ruby; me and Cliff are workin' for Eamon Mooney now. We'll be collectin' your rent. Okay?' I smiled.

'Blood-money,' spat out Ruby.

' 'Scuse me?' This was going to be painful. It was dawning on me that we might have to earn our dough.

'It's only commerce. You're runnin' a business from this shop. Eamon owns the premises.' The till shot open, Ruby yanked out a white envelope, slamming it on the counter.

'You don't need to count it. It's all there, every penny.'

'The thing is, Ruby; the rent's goin' to rise a bit this month. Thirty quid-a-week – that's £520 for a calender month,' I said, trying to clarify the new terms.

'I've always paid £390; now you come in demanding £520. I'm a widow you know, it's 33 years since my Frankie passed on,' here we go.

'This is nothing to do with me, Ruby. Yeh must 'ave known it was comin'.'

'He's got people queuin' up for places like this; he could get seven 'undred, easy.' Cliff's input did nothing to calm Ruby, she was close to tears as she parted with the balance.

'Maybe you should consider retirement, Rube. Put ya feet up?'

'Yeah, move down to Cornwall, cream teas and all that caper.'

'I love this shop. I'll die behind this counter before you lot get me out,' said Ruby melodramatically.

'No-one wants to get you out, Ruby, it's only an overdue rent increase for Christ's sake,' I explained.

'I know what Mooney's up to – don't worry about that.'

'Take care of yourself, Rube. We'll see yeh next month,' she'd already switched off, burying herself into a Mills & Boon.

Cliff draped his arms around my shoulders – 'Well, that went nice and smoothly, mate!'

'Didn't it just.' I wasn't feeling too guilty, I looked upon the money as reparations, for grassing me up when I was a kid.

'Right, let's go see the Ferret. I'm gettin' the taste for this racket,' enthused Cliff.

'If we get a result with Jimmy, I'll get yer beer in all week.'

'Too right you will.'

The drive to the Prussia was spent station-hopping with the

radio, in a fruitless effort to find a decent tune in between the drivel spewed out by the cretins loading the CDs. Unhappily, there was no Robert Elms or Peter Curran on Saturday mornings to break the cycle of senses-numbing chart pap which was released onto the airwaves of London.

Ever since I started drinking in pubs – I've been fascinated by the men who spend all-day (everyday) liquefying and picklefying their livers – plotted up in a darkened corner or recess: a breed apart, as they appear to have no need to work, eat, shop, or even spend time at home with their families. On the surface, it's a carefree, idyllic way of life. Jimmy was almost a member of this society; although I was hardly bogged down with responsibilities and commitments, the freedom these supposed misfits enjoyed, was an occasional source of envy.

The Prussia was in Turpin Road, set back from the nearby shops, situated in the less affluent part of Wapping. The superficial regeneration of the Docklands hadn't extended to the Prussia. It was much the same as it had always been – a dump. The distressed walls weren't designer.

Unlike Ruby, Jimmy was a likeable individual; the breakdown of his marriage was the catalyst for his fall from grace as a rock of the Irish 'scene' in Seven Kings. Jimmy's wife took up with a partner in the solicitors firm she worked for in Plaistow. Every one knew Jimmy, he was equipped with a sharp sense of humour and a razor tongue – and, was at one time, completely dedicated to his dance school. Carmel and Siobhan were star pupils in their youth, much to Mum's delight but, I was a disappointment. I just didn't like it, I was born twenty years too early; Irish dancing wasn't hip back then, when Punk was boiling over.

Cliff gestured towards the back of the bar. Jimmy was tucked away in the corner playing on a prehistoric one-armed bandit.

'Hope you're winnin', Jimmy?'

'Yeh couldn't win on these machines; he doctors them. Should I know you, son?'

'You tried to teach me to dance. You had more luck with Siobhan and Carmel – me sisters. They've got hundreds of medals and trophies indoors.'

'You're Patsy's lad?' said Jimmy.

'I am – Derry,' we shook hands.

'God, I remember you – yeh was feckin' hopeless; yer sisters had talent, though. I'd get yeh a pint, only I'm a bit tight this week,' as were the other 51.

'It's not a drink I'm after, Jimmy.'

'What are yeh lookin'?' said Jimmy fishing.

'We work for Eamon Mooney – collections department,' Jimmy's jaw plunged to the floor.

'Oh... that's grand,' said Jimmy unconvincingly.

'Your next payment's due Monday. You only paid £80 last month, that leaves you owin' £20 plus £40 interest, altogether, that'll make it £200 on Monday. Will you have it?' Jimmy scooped up the coins from the ledge of the one-armed bandit.

'Do yeh know what, lads, I might just squeeze a round from this, now. What'll youse have?'

'It's okay, Jimmy, Cliff'll get 'em. Pint please, mate – and one for Jimmy. How's the Guinness 'ere, Jim?'

'Great stuff, Derry. Kieran keeps the pipes spotless.'

'I thought we was s'posed to be collectin' money, not fuckin' givin' it away,' moaned Cliff as he went off to the bar cursing.

This drew a nervous smile from Jimmy, whom, I knew had money coming in. I'd been told he was working in a pallet yard in Bow.

'How's the family keepin', Derry?' With perhaps the exception of the clowns in Billy Smart's Circus, I don't think I've seen a face looking so comically sad and sorrowful. Poor Jimmy.

'Things are tickin' over, Jimmy. Everyone's keepin' busy.'

'That's what's important these days, Derry. Stop for a second an' you're dead.'

'Couldn't agree more. How yeh gettin' on down the Regency?'

'Terry pays me nothin', besides, I'm only doin' the odd day.'

Terry McGee was the owner of this royally-named business, which was buried behind the Black Lion and the deliveries entrance to Safeway's. A thriving concern, it was a mystery to me how he was able to generate so much cash trading in battered wooden pallets; Terry always held a mighty wedge in his pocket – just in case his car broke-down and he had to buy a new one – or something.

'Yeh better ask 'im for some overtime, then. I need that two 'undred on Monday. I ain't got time to keep comin' back for dribs an' drabs,' I told Jimmy.

Miraculously, Cliff set the glasses down on the table without spilling a drop – not once checking to see where the table was – his eyes zeroing-in on a stubby Blonde that came sauntering out of the loo, wrapped in a grossly unflattering leopard-skin top which was knotted above her bulging gut.

'Bit of a sort!' said Cliff admiringly.

'Yeah, the sort yeh throw rocks at.' Placing my chair beside Jimmy's, I quietly and, discreetly, put my cards on the table: 'I don't wanna start off on the wrong foot with yeh, Jimmy; this is a bad enough job to begin with. We've got too much grief in the world as it is. Know what I mean? I don't want to have a nasty relationship with anyone – especially not you.'

'I won't give yeh any trouble, Derry.' A solitary drop of stout had dripped onto Jimmy's discoloured polo shirt – which, blended in nicely with the nicotine-stained wallpaper.

Gingerly, Jimmy lifted his wallet from his back pocket: 'Here's fifty, you'll have the rest Monday,' said Jimmy gloomily.

'D'yeh want me to come to the yard?'

'No. I'll meet yeh here at lunchtime; one-ish. I don't want Terry knowin' all me business, Derry.'

'Fair enough, Jim. What's that Paxton brew like?'

'It's lethal gear, Derry – wipe out material.'

Cliff was still transfixed, staring open-mouthed at the rum old slapper sitting at the bar – feeding her grubby face with scampi à la basket.

'There's a big void in your life, Cliff,' I suggested.

'Oh yeah; 'ow's that?'

'You've no culture,' I concluded.

'I've got all the culture I need, my friend – at the end of me dick!' Cliff said proudly.

'Albert Einstein... Come-On-Down!'

'Listen to Mr MENSA, Jimmy. You're no different to me, Derry, you're just a bit more selective,' said Cliff defensively.

'I could 'ardly be less!'

'Would yeh stop talkin' about women, fellas. Youse're spoilin' me pint,' said Jimmy.

'He's after datin' a wee Donegal lassie, Jimmy,' said Cliff in an appalling Irish accent, which was more akin to an Australian Pakistani.

'They'll burn yeh, Derry. Sooner or later – they'll burn yeh.'

'I'm not exactly choosin' bridesmaids dresses yet, Jimmy.'

'Pale peach for the bridesmaids, dear,' said Cliff in a more convincing "I'm free!" voice.

Cliff's head was oscillating between me and Jimmy, and Nelly no-knickers at the bar; she was now absorbed in a futile attempt to re-fasten the buttons on her skirt and squash in her bloated belly.

We'd two more 'visits' planned for the day: Breffni Wilson (the last payment on a £200 loan), and Jack Gurley. He was a doorman at the Glenvale and had taken out a considerably bigger loan of £5,000. These two, however, were both good-payers, and I didn't anticipate any problems. I was steadily forming the opinion that this wasn't a Prohibition-type game to be ashamed of. We were merely vital cogs in a machine which was dispensing goodwill and cash, filling a gap in the Black financial market; I wasn't a 'heavie', more of a social worker.

All of these concerns were secondary to Liz; the whole of my foreseeable future was dependant on this girl. I knew she was a special person but, persuading her that I was a good-catch, too, might be difficult. Certainly it would be well-advised to be a tad economical with the truth with regards to the precise nature of my new job – at least until we get to know each other a bit better. Anyway, I'd have plenty of time to talk to Liz in the club: Saturdays were dead, always quiet, Friday was bingo night, and Sunday – everyone donned their glad rags for the big dance.

* * * * * * *

Kevin and Cliff had set off hell for leather along the M6, and were recklessly determined to reach Southport before noon, so they could revel in two days drunken debauchery at a Club 18-30 reunion bash. Martin was taking Lauren and her sister for a curry down the imaginatively-named Golden Chicken –

in what was an uncharacteristic show of perseverance given the surprising knock back he'd received on Tuesday night. Chris and Davey were on a mission of thuggery in Leicester – supposedly watching the Irons in their perennial fight against relegation.

Thus as we entered the marbled-floor portal of the club, I was reasonably confident that we wouldn't be disturbed too much. We were greeted by Brendan O'Malley, the all-powerful barsteward at the club. Brendan was catching the punters as they arrived, in an effort to extricate their membership-renewal money.

'Five pounds off yeh, Derry. You're one of the last as usual.'

'Sorry, Brendan. I thought Patsy was goin' to settle up.'

'Yeh thought wrong. He said, let the little bastard pay his own way.'

'He loves me really, Bren; 'ere, put the change in the raffle kitty.'

'Lovely, very generous,' said Brendan as he pocketed the spare fiver left from the ten-pound note.

'How'd the Line dancin' go, Brendan? Did yeh get a crowd?'

'Aye, not bad. The ol' biddies in the bingo mafia were moanin' about them takin' all the space, though,' sighed Brendan.

'They're a mean bunch, Bren. They think they own the bloody place. Yeh can't please 'em all, mate.'

'You're not jokin', I should bar the lot of 'em. Now, *who* might this ravishing vision of heaven be?' panted Brendan.

'Liz, this is Brendan – the Boss. Be careful, he'll be tryin' to poach you from the Crown. Liz works for Gerry, Bren. She's family of Noeleen's.'

'I can see she doesn't favour Gerry. You're very welcome

here, darlin',' fluttered Brendan.

'Pleased to meet yeh, Brendan.'

'Any time you need work, Liz – you know where to come.'

'Thanks. I'll remember that,' said Liz politely.

'How long are you over for, Liz?'

'I've no fixed plans. I finished my degree last year and made the decision to travel.'

'Yeh didn't get very far, pet! What was yeh studyin'?'

'Thermodynamics.'

'Sorry!?' said a baffled Brendan.

'It's a science; the relationship between heat and other forms of energy. Very intense course,' explained Liz.

'I bet. That'll come in handy down the Crown; they have a very intellectual clientèle!' smirked Brendan.

'You never told me you was a Brain, Liz.'

'Didn't wanna intimidate yeh, Derry!' laughed Liz.

'Mmm... that wouldn't take much. Shall we grab a seat?'

Slack though it was on a Saturday night, you had to be in early to claim a table. The only one left was next to the pool table. This was particularly unpleasant when Bobby Cush was playing. A repugnant turd at the best of times, you could multiply that by infinity when he was on the pool table, as he had a teeth-grinding habit of shouting 'T-I-M-B-E-R' every time he potted a ball.

'I'm on form tonight, Derry lad – they couldn't get close. No one can touch me,' blustered Bobby.

'They wouldn't wanna, yeh fuckin' eejit,' said Brendan as he swept through the tables collecting glasses.

'You're a real hustler, Bobby,' I said brightly.

'C'mon, Derry, giv'us a game. I'll go easy wit' yeh?'

'Maybe in another life, Bobby.'

'How 'bout your young lady, Derry?' begged Bobby.

'D'yeh play, Liz?'

'I'm a friggin' demon. I'll challenge yeh in that other life, Derry,' Liz winked at Bobby.

'You're on. How'll I recognize yeh, though?' I worried.

'Don't worry, *darrlin'*. I'll find yeh!' There she goes again, rolling those Rs – what a peach of a voice.

Liz went to the bar to collect our drinks after insisting she bought the first round. Surveying the tables around us, every set of male – and, female eyes, were aimed at Liz's bum. Seldom has the club witnessed such a vision: few of the regular congregation would have the balls – or the figure, to wear such provocative, skin-tight leather kecks.

It was great entertainment watching the women's faces, trying to lip-read their disapproval and indignation at the cheek of this brazen hussy, enticing their men by her very presence. The skill of lip-reading wasn't required to interpret the thoughts of the men, though; as Liz swivelled round clutching two pints of Guinness, the face-on view was awesome. Her ample bosom – firm and well-proportioned, was nonchalantly defying gravity.

'I feel like I'm in a goldfish bowl sittin' here, Derry. Have I done something wrong?' asked Liz.

'Nah. Strange faces always get the treatment,' I reassured her.

'The women behind me are givin' us some serious daggers.'

'They're wonderin' who you are, that's all,' I said lying.

'This is a grand club, mind. I didn't realize how big it was,' she said in positive admiration of the opulent refurbishment.

'Brendan saved the place. It was dyin' before he took charge. There was no live music – and worse, the beer was shit; the club was empty. How's ya Guinness?'

'It's... okay. Yeh couldn't beat the stout in Donegal, though.

Yeh should get over there and try it, Derry.'

'If that's an invitation – I accept!' Liz smiled, releasing a *Daz*-white gleam from her teeth, which was joined by a wickedly arched eyebrow.

'We've got some crackin' bars in Tyrone, too, yeh know. We'll 'ave to go on a tour an' compare notes.'

'It won't be much of a tour if Tuesday's anythin' to go by!'

'Ah c'mon, that was an exception. I didn't eat me dinner.'

Once again, Liz was panning around the club – studying the elegant decor. Although it didn't exactly rival the Taj Mahal for craftsmanship and design, it was, however, without equal amongst Irish Catholic social clubs.

'T-I-M-B-E-R,' roared Bobby.

'Sorry about that prick, Liz. He's not right in the head,' I said trying to excuse his moronic celebration.

'Looks as if he's had a fair loch o' beers.'

'You're not jokin', he never misses a session – afternoon or evening. Seven days-a-week.'

'Not married I take it?'

'Nah, he's got no family over here. There's a brother in Cork; never goes back, though.'

'That's sad but. It'll be a lonely life for him.'

'I wouldn't worry about him, Liz. He's past redemption.'

'There's hope for us all, Derry.' Liz's face was a tough one to read; piercing eyes that could freeze, were at odds to a soft mouth and warm smile.

'You're a believer, then, Liz?'

'That's a leading question, Derry. I'm no fanatic... or bigot. I go to Mass; try to be good,' said Liz raising that mischievous eyebrow again.

'Good for you, Liz.'

'Yeh must get somethin' out of the church, Derry?' ventured

Liz positively.

'I do. I love goin' to church on a cold, sunny December morning and just sitting there – watching the shafts of light bursting through the stained-glass windows like beams from a raygun. All those reds an' blues. Now that's beautiful.'

'Is that it?'

'Basically,' I confirmed.

'YES!' Walter Delay was jubilant after winning £25 on the fruit machine, holding his baseball cap aloft, and presumably expecting a flood – with his tracksuit bottoms hitched to his nipples.

'I don't go every Sunday, Liz. Besides, there's more to faith than trotting out on a Sunday mornin' to pay your covenants. I've seen it; half of 'em fly out the door once they've tossed their silver in the basket,' I said virtuously.

'Are yeh sure the truth isn't, you're sufferin' a hangover, or just too idle to get out of bed on a Sunday mornin'?'

'You been talkin' to me mum? It's like this, Liz; I'm pacin' meself. I don't wanna peak too early – I'm gettin' better as I get older. These born-do-gooders end up with all the vices goin': drinkin', drugs, gamblin' – loose-women.'

'You'll be gettin' those out the way first, then!?'

'I'm a quiet lad, Liz. Gerry might tell you a different story. It's just an impression people get – the wrong one.'

'A soul that's misunderstood, Derry?' teased Liz.

'You're a cynic, Liz. It must be the job, listenin' to all of those hard luck stories, from the drunken wretches in the Crown.'

'I'm a good judge of character, Derry. I weed out the wasters.'

'I'm frightened to ask what you think of me, then!'

'I haven't made me mind up about you, Derry. The gut feeling's promising, though!'

'Meaning?' I wanted reassurance.

'Meaning, I wouldn't be here if I wasn't sure about yeh.' Liz looked a bit embarrassed.

We were both in need of a refill – just as well, I wasn't sure where this little tête-à-tête was heading. On my way to the bar I became wary of saying too much or the wrong thing to Liz. As he pulled the pints, Brendan was gazing at Liz – she'd struck up a conversation with the women behind us who'd been eyeballing her, and, within seconds, converted her would-be antagonists.

'I've one question for yeh, Derry. What would a girl like Liz be doin' with a shameless reprobate like you.. it can't be your money?' surmised Brendan jealously.

'Charisma, matey,' I replied assuredly.

'Charisma!! You've got about as much charisma as a Venetian blind. It must be something else?'

'You're right. My drama teacher at school said I had the look of a young Montgomery Clift – dreamy... moody. What d'yeh reckon, Bren?'

'Yeah, I can see that, Derry. Who's Montgomery Clift?' Brendan always did that, he'd nod in agreement, then, when you'd finished speaking, ask what you was talking about.

'He's an actor, Bren.'

'Gotcha. One of the soaps?'

'He's dead, Bren.'

'That's desperate. Everyone seems to be dying these days; look at Eamon Andrews.'

'Yep, he's dead.' I escaped from the vacuous chat with Brendan and took the Guinness over to Liz. Bobby Cush was still showing off, swaggering around the pool table twirling his cue like a majorette. I was willing the finely sculptured alabaster bust of Fearghal O'Riordan's head (Life-President and first Chairman of the club) to drop from its lofty perch and kill him.

'There yeh go, Liz. *Sláinte!*'

'*Sláinte*, Derry,' clink.

'I see you broke the ice with Mrs Rouney.'

'God, yeh know, Derry, she's very nice. Said you should bring me to the dance on Sunday,' Liz was sounding more comfortable.

'I doubt if it would be your scene, Liz. They're a bit behind the times here... old-fashioned. The music's hardly likely to send you into a frenzied fit of rapture, it's all that old slow stuff; one-two-three, one-two-three.'

'I luv that dancin', Derry. You need to be very light on yer feet but, it's very skilful,' said Liz exuberantly.

'To be honest, Liz, I wouldn't associate anyone in this club with the word skilful.. sinful maybe. Your life's in danger if you try an get past 'em with a drink in ya hand, they've no control.'

'Do *you* do a turn on the floor, Derry?'

'I beg your pardon, missus!?'

'You're a terrible bad man, Derry. Dancin', I meant *dancin'!*'

'Oh, I see. Well... yeah, if someone makes me an offer I can't refuse.'

'What if I were to make you an offer yeh can't refuse Sunday night?' proposed Liz.

'I could be tempted. I've got a late start Monday, anyway.'

'Will we bring Luke?'

'Luke, are you sure? He goes dinlo when 'e hears the band start playin'. He'll toss yeh from one end of the hall to the other, Liz. He's a strong little bugger.'

'Catch yourself on, Derry, I'm a lot tougher than I look. I'll take care of Luke. No problem.'

'Well, he loves comin' down here, I know that. Trouble is, me mum an' dad might be down here tomorrow night.'

'That's great. I'd like to meet them, Derry.'

'It'll be awkward, Liz, you won't be able to breathe. They'll be givin' you the Spanish Inquisition. The ol' man'll be tracin' your ancestors back to the Famine.'

'I like to meet people, Derry. It's what life's all about. Be nice to say hello at least. I like to see what people are really like, and how their personality was shaped; meetin' their parents usually gives a biggish clue!' Liz screwed up her eyes and fixed me with an interrogating stare.

'It's a date. Don't say I didn't warn you, though,' I said with a hint of a threat.

'Are yeh workin' tomorrow, Derry?'

'I don't work Sundays, Liz. We take Luke swimming.'

'We?'

'Cliff always comes with us.'

'Always?'

'He never misses. D'yeh fancy goin'?'

'Swimming's not my specialist subject, but I could do with the exercise like. Yeh know?'

'I don't think I've ever seen a girl who needs exercise less, mate (a bit of toffee can be very effective!).'

'C'mon, Derry, you'll have me blushin'. But I'll tell yeh, I need to get fit. Workin' behind a bar's not great for your health.'

'Yeah, you should get out of the pub game. Get back into that Thermos-flask thing.'

'Thermodynamics, Derry.'

'Right.'

'There's no rush. Like I said, I enjoy meeting people. A

career isn't the be-all and end-all.'

'Spoken like a true student!' I joked.

'What's that s'posed to mean, then?' Liz took umbrage.

'Nothin', really. But, why bother with all the books and all the studyin' in the first place?' I asked reasonably.

'Are yeh fuckin' jokin', Derry? The Rathmullan Democrat's job section takes up about three lines. Our Tarrah applied for a job as a checkout-girl at Dempsey's supermarket – and she got it. D'yeh know how many people applied for that fuckin' job? Fifteen hundred. Fifteen hundred for a friggin' checkout-girl's job,' Liz exploded.

'I was pullin' ya leg, Liz. I know what it's like there. Jobs or no-jobs, education's a good thing. Me? I had fuck-all. And it shows. It's different over here, though – there's tons of jobs. Students here use it as an excuse – to bum around for five years and hide from the real world.'

'What's wrong with that?' demanded Liz.

'Nothing. But I'm glad they cut their grants. Let 'em buy their own fuckin' books.'

'Come down off that soapbox, Derry, and get me a vodka'n'coke. I've no room left for any more Guinness.' Liz slipped me a tenner from her purse before heading off to the ladies'.

3. REAL LIFE

I was adjusting the driving mirror as I made my way to the Crown to meet Liz – watching the silent passenger in the back. Luke was staring into space.

'What's up, mate?' I asked in a soft tone.

'Nothing. I'm just lookin' at the sky.' Luke was an accurate gauge for determining the quality of a person's character. A few minutes observing somebody talking to Luke, or just being around him, was usually enough to tell if they were of a good heart and sound mind –not that I had any doubt with the calibre of Liz. Even so, it was reassuring to see her return Luke's bear hug with such gusto and power. Luke was visibly shaken by the strength of this slight-framed female. For me and Luke, this was evidence absolute of her class.

For the first time in years Cliff dropped out of swimming. He came out with some crap about not wanting to play gooseberry. He was jealous of Liz being invited along for a swim – he'd built a close relationship with Luke which he was justifiably proud of.

My bond with Cliff was cemented at St. Peter's Junior School, in Whitechapel. I strolled into the playground bog and found him being bullied out of his chip money by Gary Burns, a most ugly specimen, and the best fighter in the school. Burns was slapping Cliff around, but there was no obvious reason for me to risk life-and-limb by intervening. To this day, I'm not sure why I did kick him in the back of the knee with my monkey boots; he went down like a sack-of-shit, smashing his head on a urinal. His nut split open like the peach in the 'Think Bike!' road safety advert. Twenty-five stitches later, we were both suspended for two weeks – and, at the age of ten, the rot had set-in on our less than mediocre academic careers.

I switched the car-radio on and caught the end of 'Money's Too Tight To Mention' – repeat to fade: *'Did the earth move for yeh Nancy? Did the earth move for yeh Nancy?'*

Swimming-pools to the majority of the populace, are simply a public facility you occasionally visit to lark about or take a swim. Not to me, though – I love the very fabric of the building: the charmless cubicles in the regimented changing-rooms, the unpalatable fare criminally displayed in the cafe, and the confused identity of the soup in the vending machine. I drown myself in the tranquillity of the non-atmosphere that exists inside the pool, which always sends me into a dream-like trance once the chlorine has invaded my pores. Even a recent violent experience of 'Swimming-lane Rage' hadn't dampened my passion.

A cluster of simpletons huddled together beneath the diving boards – Liz was looking at me looking at them, as they gleefully ridiculed Luke, who was oblivious to their scorn.

'They're worthless, Derry. Worth nothin'. Luke's already ten times the man they'll ever grow up to be,' said Liz trying to calm and comfort me. Mistakenly, she expected an aggressive response.

'Don't worry, Liz. It doesn't bother me, and it doesn't bother Luke. It's a common reaction; people try to boost their own self-esteem by belittling the likes of Luke, who, they perceive to be weaker or a lesser person. Anyone that's a bit fatter, or a bit uglier than the norm – they all get stick, it's human nature,' I said philosophically.

'That's a very mature way to deal with rubbish like them, so it is, Derry.'

'Not really. Besides, if they'd been a bit bigger I'd of lost it, and battered 'em.' If I was being honest, I did it all the time as well – even with Luke. Not to his face, obviously, or in any tangible or nasty way, but in my head, I'd strengthen my own ego by comparing our lives – the almost boundless freedom I had, against Luke's semi-caged, supervised world. Who was actually the happiest with their lot, however, was a close call, with the educated chips stacked on Luke's number.

Luke was already cavorting around in the water like a crazed dolphin with a poisoned harpoon stuck in its trap; Liz and I were dipping our toes tentatively, resembling a pair of old grannies paddling on Worthing beach.

'Get you in there, Derry. I thought yeh said, yeh swam like a fish?' said Liz reminding me of the previous night's boasting session.

'I do, I do. Not all fish swim like fishes, though... yeh know?'

'See you, Derry – it's statements like that which gives the Irish a bad name!'

'C'mon, Liz, this is ridiculous. All you've got to do, is to imagine it's a brilliant summer's day, and you're standing on the bank of the Liffey. The government's just drained the river and filled it with Gerry's Guinness, perfectly chilled, for some publicity – to bring the Yanks in.'

'Flip me, Derry. That's not a bad idea, fella!' I could fight the urge no longer. Instinctively, I grasped Liz's flawless, silken flesh – one hand around her calf, the other just above her derrière, and, before giving a fleeting manic grin, launched her (screaming) into the deep-end.

'Yeh bugger, Derry – it's freezin'!' Liz barely had a chance to squirt out a mouthful of water, before Luke plunged her back down to the bottom. Gallantly, if a touch late, I dived in with Johnny Weissmuller-conviction, to save the day.

'LUKE! What you playin' at, yeh daft bastard? She's a girl; it's not Cliff you're muckin' about with, now.' Liz resurfaced behind Luke and lifted herself onto his shoulders – and successfully sank him. Game on, the next hour flew. Left as a bystander, I watched from the side, as the pair of them bobbed up-and-down, chasing each other through the water. They were getting on great, which triggered a curious pattern of thoughts: would Liz be able to cope with Luke as a permanent fixture? Could I? What if Mum and Dad were suddenly struck down with Alzheimer's Disease, how would we manage?

Concern about which of the siblings would make the ultimate sacrifice, and dedicate their time to being a nursemaid for Luke, was hardly pressing, still, the form guide was thus: Siobhan was a non-starter – too feckless, Carmel was the sensible and, more practical option, but I was closer to Luke.

Children afflicted by autism are inevitably cocooned by their families in a protective web, which all good parents (disability or not) entangle their kids in – at least until they reach the late-teens. Luke, however, would never escape the family net – ever, unless of course, he were to be institutionalized. Mum once told me, that she didn't expect me, Siobhan or Carmel to take responsibility for Luke after we were married: 'Taking care of your own wife and children is all I'd ever ask of yeh, Derry. Luke's my son; my baby.' – 'Don't be silly, Mum,' I said. The truth is, I was employing my racehorse blinkers, as I generally did when attempting to block out some inexorable fact – like going on the piss in Tenerife with Martin and Kevin when there was no money in the bank and no credit on the credit cards. The ritual descent into abject misery which follows the opening of the 'brown envelopes' could, without exception, always wait for another week.

Liz breaststroked her way to the side of the pool where I

stood waiting, and shook her jet-black locks vigorously as she climbed the steps. Then she hit me with a honeyed-smile.

'Giv'us a towel, Derry. That boy's deadly craic. I'm shattered! Where's he get the energy from?' As Liz dried her stiffening limbs, I pretended to be listening intently, though, not a single word she uttered was absorbed or digested; I was visiting another planet entirely.

Luke sprang out of the water and barged in between us.

'Derry, can we marry Liz?' The meeting of eyes was broken by Liz smothering Luke with her towel.

'I think he likes you, Liz,' I said stating the obvious.

'Ah, bless 'im, he doesn't know what I'm really like!' kidded Liz as she dried Luke's hair.

'Can we go in the cafe, Derry?' asked Luke eagerly.

'Yeah. What yeh gonna have?'

'Vinegar and chips and a blue Slush.'

'Excellent combination.'

* * * * * * *

The scheduled meet-the-parents ordeal, was thankfully put off. Patsy caught a dose of the flu and fled to his bed, looking so resplendent in his silky jimjams, which were supplied by Siobhan for his fiftieth birthday.

Cliff was mad for business, and, following Eamon's orders, kitted himself out with a natty whistle from Mister Byrite's – 'It's a matter of respect, fellas. The manner in which you carry yourself is paramount – look at me. You are what you wear. A suit gives you dignity and presence – they love to see yeh wearin' one when you're collecting their money.' The gospel according to Eamon Mooney, and worringly, he truly believed 'the suit' would somehow numb the pain they felt, when we relieved them of their meagre pittance.

Cliff was bending down, checking the cut of his cloth in the few clear inches of mirror between the optics and the bar. This was our first proper day with Eamon, but we had to begin proceedings in the Crown – to celebrate the dawn of a new era.

'Yeh look like a prize-winnin' turkey, yeh thick bollock. Where d'yeh think ya goin' dressed like that?' asked Gerry.

'Businessmen, Gerry... Dress like this,' reported Cliff.

'Have yeh bang'd ya head, boy? Have yeh been in an accident? Swear to God, you'll be carryin' a briefcase next,' said Gerry struggling to come to terms with the metamorphosis in Cliff's appearance.

'He looks the part, though. Don't yeh think?' I appealed on Cliff's behalf.

'He looks like a bloody encyclopaedia salesman, Derry. Michael Jackson dresses his chimpanzee in better suits than he's wearin'. What is it youse are up to anyway?' asked Gerry with suspicion in his eyes.

'Er...' Joe McArdle intervened before I was able to muster up a plausible lie.

'Do I look alright, Derry? Feeling a bit rough to be honest with yeh; but yeh know me, Derry – don't yeh? Don't yeh, son? I used to be a serviceman; I was in the Queen's Navy, Derry,' Joe explained to me.

'You did tell me that, Joe,' I acknowledged, as I waited for his regular follow-up line.

'Look at these hands; they've seen action. But I always look smart, Derry. You know I always look smart, Derry,' added Joe.

'You always look smart, Joe,' I agreed.

Joe was harmless, drunk just enough to keep himself in a liquid-fuelled haze, thereby facilitating his fluent gibberish.

He'd make the same point, over and over. Last week it was Waterloo Bridge: 'Waterloo Bridge was built by women during the war yeh know? I'm tellin' yeh; it was built by women during the war,' not that anyone was arguing – or listening. If I was deep in thought, Joe was annoying; almost as annoying as watching Loyd Grossman fiddling about at the red table on *MasterChef*, whilst the food on the yellow and blue tables went cold.

Gerry had moved on, buzzing from customer to customer. Liz and Noeleen were away shopping for groceries and Karen was nowhere to be seen.

'Where's Karen, Harry?' I enquired.

'She's gone away,' was his brief answer.

'How long for?' I persisted.

'For as long as you've got a hole in yer arse. Gerry sacked her last night.'

'What for?'

'She wasn't puttin' all the money in the till,' said Harry.

'Who told you that?'

'Gerry told me – she was robbin' him blind.'

'You sure? She seemed straight as a post, Karen,' I remained unconvinced of her guilt.

'She's a tea leaf, Derry; which makes a change from that stingy bastard muggin' us – two pound an' six-pence for a pint of bloody stout he's chargin'.'

'Make you right, Harry; at least Dick Turpin had the courtesy to wear a mask.'

Gerry ghosted up behind Harry and me, ready to leap into the conversation: 'I hope yeh won't be takin' up too much of Liz's valuable time, Derry; now that we're short on labour?' Gerry asked.

'I'm busy meself at the moment, Gerry. Socializing can wait.'

'She's been singin' your praises to Noeleen – said you're a real Gentleman.' I waited patiently for the rub; Gerry having adopted the maddening practice of taking lengthy, dramatic pauses mid-sentence, before delivering the final sting.

'Noeleen's very fond of Liz, Derry; thinks an awful lot of that girl,' he said finishing with a Jack Palance-stare to emphasise the point.

'That makes two of us, then,' I returned his steely glare.

'Fine,' said Gerry.

'That was a bit naughty, the business with Karen. What a shock.'

'Terror,' Gerry shook his head.

'You'll be needin' to get a replacement fast, Gerry. You better get yourself down the Job Centre,' quipped Harry.

'I'll take your advice when I fuckin' ask for it,' barked Gerry as he snatched Harry's empty glass.

'Talkin' about staff, Gerry. Our Carmel's lookin' for a part time job; few evenings-a-week, after she gets finished at the travel agents.'

'Sure, she's no experience, Derry.'

'She'd be sweet as a nut, Gerry. At least she's honest,' I said championing the family cause.

'True. Tell her to come and see me tonight.'

'You havin' another, Derry?' offered Harry.

'Shouldn't really, I'm drivin'. Yeah, go-on,' I capitulated immediately.

'CLIFF?' yelled Harry across the pub, shaking his hand in a drinking motion.

Cliff looked over at me – 'We stayin'?' he mouthed – 'Quick one. Rapido,' I said. Some chance.

Already, I began to wonder if we possessed the essential discipline required to make a success of the opportunity handed to us by Eamon. Neither of us were especially work-oriented; in fact, Cliff, quite the contrary, and I was willingly led astray at the slightest opening.

True to form, the second pint turned into a third and the clock had yet to pass 12.30, so I chose the only sensible course of action available – a plate of beef sandwiches, with onions and mustard on crusty-white bread. Cliff sidled up beside me with a leviathan-size grin on his face, feeling chuffed, safe in the knowledge that today was already a potential write-off.

'Yeh was sayin' about this new job, Derry.' Gerry was back on my trail again.

'What's that, Gerry?' I said avoiding his gaze.

'The job you and Cliff are dressing up like *Laurel and Hardy* for,' said Gerry elucidating.

'Oh, right.' Magic! Liz and Noeleen arrived on cue with the groceries.

''Ere, Noeleen, giv'us that. I'll take it through for yeh,' I volunteered.

'Good lad, Derry,' said Noeleen unaware of the ulterior motive behind the gesture.

'Ladies,' said Cliff greeting Liz and Noeleen, before draining his glass and burping loudly.

'Excuse you, and your rude manners,' said Noeleen lifting the bar-hatch.

'Hi, Derry,' said Liz, her perfume hung in the air, a scent from a Gaelic utopia.

Liz and Noeleen came out of the kitchen whooping and hooting in a cliquey-way, with Noeleen's dirty cackle silencing the stoolies (the punters who clung to their barstools with caveman-like tenure), as they ruminated whether they were the butt of her joke. Liz did her best to straighten her face, but failed to subdue a smirk, as she rubbed her hands together.

'Right, lads. Who's waitin'?'

'Yeh can sort me and Derry, Liz. Stick one in the bin for 'Arry as well,' coughed Cliff.

'Thought yeh had a heavy day planned, Derry; wasn't expecting you in,' said Liz setting two Guinness taps running.

'We popped in for a bit of grub, Liz,' I explained.

'Monday's always our busiest day, Liz. Hellish mornin',' said Cliff.

'You're a powerful-strong liar, Cliff,' said Liz flicking the taps off.

Noeleen placed the sandwiches on the bar: 'How's your mum and dad keepin', Derry?'

'Great form, Noeleen. Thanks.'

'Good. Young Luke?'

'Really well; had a brilliant time with Liz down the baths on Sunday.'

'I heard, Derry. The poor girl was exhausted when she got home. The food's paid for, Derry,' winked Noeleen.

'No, Noeleen, come 'ere, I've got it,' I said fumbling for a fiver amidst the screwed up bits of paper with redundant phone numbers on, and the worthless receipts I kept in my black-suede bomber-jacket.

Gerry caught sight of this non-transaction and looked suitably aggrieved at the slice of profit surrendered by Noeleen.

'You had one eye in the mirror and you watched yourself go by,' indeed I did. Liz was tunefully singing along to Carly Simon, one of her jukebox selections, although I don't think she was directing the verse at me. Substituting singing for whistling, Liz wiped the bar and was confronted by Harry, who, having rejoined the fray, was desperate to entice her into performing a duet.

'Come over 'ere, gorgeous.' Harry launched into a raucous

din of jumbled melodies, finishing with the words: *'Take me back to the one that I love... Dublin... Dubberlin.'*

'Harry, you're a fuckin' blue-chip pain in the arse. How could I ever sing with yeh? You're singin' four different songs at the same time!' remarked Liz.

'Hey, did you happen to see the most beautiful girl in the world,' Harry wouldn't be silenced.

Joe was still rabbiting on like a two-bob watch, trying to elicit a response from someone. The Guinness was disappearing too quickly; there was no appetite for work now. I couldn't even be bothered to take the time and delve into my mental filing cabinet of original or, more importantly, semi-believable reasons, for not chasing a single debtor, to face Eamon with.

'Who owns this?' asked Liz holding aloft a stale pint of cider.

'It's Alfie's,' said Joe. 'He's nipped into the bookies.'

'He's been gone the best part of two hours but. What on earth does he find to do in there?' wondered Liz.

'He's chorin' all the pens; sells 'em down Romford Market for five-pence each,' suggested Harry.

'He's probably shoppin' for your Christmas present, Liz; some tasteful lingerie,' quivered Cliff.

'Ah, fuck off, Cliff,' said Liz.

'That's tidy language from a lady,' said Cliff in mock-outrage.

'Anyway, yeh know I don't wear 'em!' added Liz with juju allure.

'Charmin'. 'Ark at her; I'm O'Grady, *fly me,*' replied Cliff.

A time-check on my old watch, donated by grandad Sheehan, said ten-to-four. Bloody thing never worked more than a few minutes at a go, but it was a princely-looking set of cogs. The authentic Greenwich Mean Time was 2pm and

Jimmy Wild would more than likely be drinking his loan-payment in a less conspicuous boozer than the Prussia. Why worry? A luscious female had just entered the premises, decked out in a stylish pinstripe-jacket, with a matching miniskirt.

'Derry, check the size of her tits,' gasped Cliff.

'Christ, her Wonderbra's earning its wages,' I observed from a technical perspective.

'Look at 'em, though. They're perfect, just the right size,' said Cliff frothing

'What size is that?'

'FUCKIN' MASSIVE!' roared Cliff.

Cliff had one of those all-singing, all-dancing personalities that entertained with the explosive-bang of an Air Bomb Repeater, but equally, for some people, lost its appeal just as quickly as a firework. To the pretentiously lofty, like Nancy, he was an uncouth bore, with transparent patter, but I loved the transient quality of his friendship.

The downside of an afternoon-session in the Crown, was having to tolerate the presence of Darren and Trevor. Their life was spent flitting back and forth between the Crown and the betting shop, placing ridiculously weeny bets. Their craving for quoting endless, inane, meaningless odds at each other was insatiable; they could colloquy themselves into a coma with their insipid prattle, safe in the knowledge, no sane human being would, by choice, share more than 5-seconds with either of them. It was at times such as this, when you questioned the veracity of an Almighty Creator – and, where a duo of oddities, like Darren and Trevor, could possibly fit into his Grand Plan. They sat at their table, in the left-hand corner of the bar. Trevor had a full beard and an unbearably smug grin; a right ponce, one of those people who read the newspaper from the front. Darren was fiftyish, well-groomed, *nicely* dressed, and nodded in agreement with whatever Trevor said or proposed. His head was an empty box. Both loved their mums dearly and were safe with children. However, if anything was going to drive me out of the Crown this afternoon, it would be them.

Is There Life Before Death? Notorious Belfast graffiti, which Darren and Trevor's twilight-zone existence presented a definitive answer to. Salvation is almost free, though. I stuck a shiny nugget in the jukebox and waited impatiently for my song.

'I would go out tonight, but I haven't got a stitch to wear, this man said "it's gruesome, that someone so handsome should care".'

Morrissey/Marr

'Och, yeh wouldn't bother just. The little frigger's a demon.' Noeleen wasn't having it. Liz was endeavouring to offer a crumb of support towards Karen.

'Could've been a mistake, Noeleen. Or just the once; for bills like. She was great with her kids but. I used to see them over the park. Played with 'em for ages – yeh know? *Really* played with 'em. Not just pushing swings sayin', yeah, yeah, anytime they asked her somethin'.'

'I'm not disputin' she's a good mummy to her children, Liz; but this is our livin', pet. And you know it's hard work. If Karen's got problems, she has her own family to turn to. Anyway, Liz, what's *your* man up to; has he no work to go to?'

'Wha' d'yeh mean, Noeleen, *my* man. I hardly know the fella.'

'Liz, you've been droolin' since we came in now. Don't you try an' tell me any different but.'

'Och, Noeleen, giv'us a chance to breathe!'

'He's a good lad, Liz. You could do a terrible lot worse than Derry, so yeh could. I've known him from a wee ba; he's from a very decent family.'

'GOD! Noeleen, will yeh take a break from yourself!?'

'Watch that other spacer, mind; Cliff. That one's as queer as a bottle o' chips – dangerous critter but.'

Cliff looked worried – 'Conor Devlin's in, Derry. Eamon's told him to come and find us,' Cliff announced.

'What did yeh tell 'im we was doin' in 'ere?' I asked without thinking.

'What d'yeh think I said? It's our first day, so we thought we'd get ratarsed and fuck the job off altogether.'

'Cliff?' I persisted.

'Told 'im we was 'avin' some munch. Okay?' Cliff gave a false smile to supplement his reply.

'I can't believe he's trackin' us already. How would he know we ain't showed up anywhere yet?' I pondered.

'He's a slippery fuck, that's how. Yeh don't make the money he's made by lettin' the likes of us mug you off.'

'It's probably nothing; just wants to see us. Where's Con now?'

'He's away. We've gotta meet Eamon at Kiefer's.'

'When?'

'Now.'

'Can you drive?' Cliff never refused.

'Yeah. Come on, let's go,' Cliff lifted his jacket from the back of a chair, picking a few hairs off the collar.

I made eye contact with Liz. 'Liz, I'll see-yeh later.'

'What's the rush, Derry?'

'Got to have a look at a job for a friend. A bit of business.'

'Well, you can't stay in the pub all day, Derry. You'll have people talkin' about yeh.' Liz looked sad to see me leaving.

'That's one thing I don't worry about, Liz.'

'How far you goin'?' I knew where this was heading.

'East Ham.'

'You're not drivin', Derry; you've had five pints.'

'Nah. We're gettin' a cab,' she didn't believe me.

'I'll ring it; wait there.'

'I'm goin' home first, Liz. Thanks anyway.'

'It's no trouble.' Liz had a disconcerting way of looking deep into your eyes, without blinking or glancing away. Yet, it didn't make me feel insecure or awkward, though. I just went weak at the knees and kept my eyes glued to hers. I'd never really looked at a woman's face the way I studied Liz's – it's not something you do. What seemed like an hour was, in reality, a few seconds and I feared the 'moment' might not re-occur. Every cliché in the book applied. The last thing I was in the mood for now, was an intense meeting with Eamon: nuclear war, cancer, Third World starvation, a computerization of the planet – could concern everyone else. But not me.

* * * * * * *

The local anaesthetic actuated by the Guinness ensured that the wall-of-death drive to Kiefer's was a delightsome blur – Cliff could of driven blindfolded along the pavement on East Ham High Street and my heart wouldn't have exceeded a hundred beats per minute.

Cliff couldn't have parked much closer if he'd of ploughed straight through Kiefer's shopfront and collided with the vat of liquor sat on the back-counter. Our *Starsky and Hutch* arrival was spied by Eamon from his usual vantage point.

'It would of been too much to ask you to park discretely round the back of the shops,' I taunted.

'Yes, it fuckin' would've been,' Cliff threw the car keys at me and bounced into Kiefer's to meet Eamon.

'Have yeh had a productive morning, Cliff?' Eamon was watching me as he spoke to Cliff.

Bernie was busy refilling the brand-name sauce bottles with a low-priced substitute.

'You eatin', Derry,' asked Bernie, licking a dollop of brown sauce off the side of a bottle.

'You're alright, Bernie. You carry on, mate. I'm just gonna get some coffee. D'yeh want one, Eamon?'

'*I* don't need one, Derry,' was his cutting response.

I stirred the coffee from behind the protective haven of the counter, evaluating Eamon's state of mind: to bullshit or not to bullshit, that was the question. Eamon's maxim for life was 'money talks, bullshit walks'. He loved to recite this adage when exhorting the power of hard cash.

'Come and sit next to Eamon, Derry,' said Eamon pulling the vacant chair close to his.

I confronted Eamon with a brassy smile – 'You're lookin' well, boss. Was yeh playin' golf this mornin'?'

'I was indeed, Derry. 82, should've been 81; a bloody squirrel fell out the tree at the ninth green as I swung the putter.'

'Did he hurt himself?' Cliff's concern for the squirrel's well being was ignored by Eamon, aside from an unamused shake of the head.

'Very fair, Eamon; very fair. Who'd yeh play with?' I enquired with fake interest in my eyes.

'Mickey Irvine from the Bear. Knows how to dress that fella. Wore a lovely sweater and slacks, so he did; cherry-red.'

'Cherry-red slacks?'

'Just the jersey, Derry. The trousers were a kind of black'n' white check.' Eamon's description of Mickey's golf-clobber was voiced with serious, professional admiration.

'Inspired colour co-ordination. Did he beat you, Eamon?'

'Go 'way, Derry. He's got the best set of clubs money can buy and a rare umbrella – only, he plays golf like he runs his pub; crooked. Shot about a hundred-an'-fifty.'

'I don't get golf. All that walkin' and dodgy polo-necks,' said Cliff confused.

'What's wrong with walking? Can yeh not get ya head around the concept of exercise?' Eamon asked Cliff.

'It's fuckin' borin'. What else d'yeh need to know?' argued Cliff, as he counted the spoons of sugar he put into his coffee.

'... And you'd rather be doing?'

'Living,' said Cliff drily.

Eamon thought about Cliff's retort for a few seconds. *'Living* requires funding, Cliff. You've some money for me, Derry?'

'Course; we covered a lot of ground today – there's a monkey, there, Eamon. We're on our way to see Galaxy from 'ere.' Cliff gawped dumbfounded at the roll of notes bound by an elastic band which I slid across the table.

'First class, Derry. Galaxy's been playin' me up recently. I've chased the bastard all over Stratford. Have you arranged to meet him?'

'Not exactly. But I'll find 'im,' I said convincingly.

'I believe yeh will, Derry,' Eamon's growing faith in me, gave me a *Ready-Brek* glow. Even though the morning's work was fabricated, I took pleasure from his approval.

Hard rain was hammering down onto the street and an elderly couple sought refuge in Kiefer's doorway.

'You'd think they'd come in and buy a tea at least. They make the place look like a bloody soup kitchen,' said Eamon being his customary benevolent self.

'You'll be gettin' old yourself one day, Eamon. You might need a good Samaritan, too. Look at 'em, they'll both be pushin' up daisies before long.'

'That's fine'n'dandy, Cliff. But I don't work for the social services – this place is losin' money faster than the Royal Opera House. Who pays my bills? Not the soddin' Lottery, I know,' said Eamon indignant at the lack of government investment not being pumped into his quaint eatery.

'Did you apply to 'em?' asked Cliff.

'Aye, I'm just finalizin' the application now. I'll take the Youth off the streets and giv'em something to live for. Recreational pursuits with their pie'n'mash.'

'Recreational pursuits?' I invited Eamon to expand.

'I'll get some o' them Space Invader machines.'

'Fuckin' Space Invaders! What century did you beam down from?' Cliff was close to choking on his coffee, with the watery-brown liquid dribbling from his lips onto the table.

'See that ol' boy's coat, Cliff? It's a Burberry; now, that's a two-hundred pound coat. Are you tellin' me he can't afford to buy the old dear a bit o' grub? These pensioners hoard their money and I'm payin' for their bloody bus passes and God knows what else,' said Eamon throwing his hands up in the air in dismay.

'That boy there's probably wiped out a dozen Germans, Eamon. Can you imagine his experiences – the sacrifice?'

'Sure, what did the Germans ever do to me, Derry? Remember that ol' Mercedes coupé? It was the best car I ever owned; beautiful piece of engineering. Thirty years old, and not a dot of rust on her,' Eamon reminisced.

'Granted they make a solid motor car, but the fuckers still needed their wings clippin'. Go-on, invite 'em in for a meal.'

'I will certainly, Derry. You can pay.'

Bernie was hovering by our table, messing about with the sauce bottles, and I could tell he was eager to speak with me –

the forgotten makeover of his bathroom was likely to be top of the agenda.

'Are you okay there, Bernie?'

'To tell yeh the truth, Derry, I'm not. Rita's givin' me no peace at all. You said you'd phone me – about the bathroom. Get the Portuguese tiles, no expense spared; I don't care any more. She's drivin' me nuts.'

'What the hell's she frettin' about, Bernie? The bathroom's fine as it is. She'll be lookin' gold taps next,' Eamon didn't like the idea of spending money on properties he owned, even though it was Bernie's money.

'Yeh know what she's like, Eamon. It's that bloody *Hello!* magazine fillin' her head with notions. She's seen Joan Collins' toilet.' Bernie was drained of resistance.

'I feel sorry for you, Bernie; lettin' a woman trample all over yeh like that. Where's your pride, man?' said Cliff adopting a bulldog stance.

'Look at you; Warren Beatty,' muttered Bernie, as he set about tackling the salt and pepper pots.

'I'll 'ave to sort the poor bastard out,' I said to no-one in particular.

'Would you take me to the airport Friday mornin', Derry? I'm goin' home for the weekend,' said Eamon.

'Yeah, course. Stanstead?'

'Yeah. Nancy's a bit tied up.' Nancy was always a bit tied up; buzzing to and fro in her tiny Fiat sports car. Not looking after children or anything so mundane as that – they didn't have any. Eamon told me they'd been trying for five years with no luck, and that Nancy was pushing for fertility treatment. Eamon wasn't too keen, though. He'd already seen three sons hatched from his first marriage and was stalling Nancy. She, however, needed kids. They were the only accessory she was missing – and she felt like an outcast when the young, well-toned mums with flat stomachs and pierced belly buttons started boasting about their babies. The gym was a cruel place.

4. 999

Morning has broken. The Sun was peeping at me through a slit in the lime-green corduroy curtains which, unsurprisingly, were left behind by the previous owners of our house. The initial feeling to creep over me was depression; not in itself rare but, on *this* morning, well justified. Apart from the usual hassles – waking up; wash; breakfast, I had to set about retrieving the £500 which I'd foolishly given to Eamon. This had been entrusted to me by my mother, to pay for Luke's exchange-visit to an American family, organised by Barronmead. Luke was flying off to Detroit with a delegation of sixteen fellow students and five teachers.

While I reflected on the error of my ways, Mum's knock on the door galvanized me into action (I opened my eyes).

'It's seven, Derry. What time have yeh to be workin'?'

'I'm gettin' up now, Mum.'

'You havin' a fry?'

'No. Can you put the coffee pot on, three cups.' Three cups of 'Colombian' and two Marlboro Lights, should be sufficient to kick-start any potentially stress-filled day. I booted the duvet off the bed and smiled back at Dennis Wise, who had prime spot on my bedroom door. Last night's clothes were set in a heap on the floor. Irritated that I hadn't taken the time to hang the suit up, I threw the bundle of designer threads into the wardrobe: this was a jeans and black crew-neck jumper day.

Chris Evans was all around me, his breakfast show was seeping out from under the bathroom door; Siobhan was locked in. Finbarr brushed past me on the stairs, barking savagely and indiscriminately. A Staffordshire Bull Terrier – and, pound-for-pound, the hardest dog in the road. He breezed in through the back door one morning with Dad, who'd just come off a night shift. A Galway man at the foundry, Devlin, threatened to poison his *Chum* and dump him in the Thames, so Patsy took pity on his tattered coat. The clattering noise made by his paws on the bare floorboards and stairs reverberated all over the house, as we awaited fitting of the new carpets. None of us paid him much attention, but he was an accepted member of the Sheehan family.

The lounge door was ajar, with the cathode ray tube emitting electrons to an empty room. The television was switched on at breakfast, and left on, regardless to whether anyone was actually watching it. Mum didn't like the house to be *too* quiet, so the telly was left running till the last person went to bed. An aromatic smell of roasted beans aroused my nostrils – smoking away in the kitchen, the percolator was a lifeline; it was a premature wedding gift from a near-fatal relationship, from my not-so-distant past.

Elanor Hughes and I *almost* walked the aisle. Almost, is maybe too strong a word, as indeed, is relationship; a euphemism I employed to give legitimacy to the two vapid years I spent webbed up with Elanor. She accused me of a most heinous crime: 'You selfish bastard, Derry. You think I'm some subservient animal, to be at your beck and call (er... yeah), ready and willing, for when your mates haven't got any money left to piss-it-up with you in the Crown.' The heinous crime? The suggestion that I would only drink with my mates when *they* had money. She didn't understand, probably never would.

In fact, the cement which held us together for two years

was Elanor's father, Barry, a celebrated musician from Sligo, who could play some killer tunes on the mandolin. More recently, though, he had established himself in the greyhound world, as a top-flight, trainer-owner. We'd go racing twice a week, at Romford and Walthamstow dogtracks. I still went with him on Thursdays to Walthamstow, we got on famously, also, I saw him most days in the Crown. Elanor was different, however; she held me in contempt, pure hatred. I briefly flirted with the idea of marrying her just for Barry's sake, didn't want to offend him, but that would of been the only reason, since I'd already taken custody of the percolator.

'Have some toast with your coffee, Derry,' Mum put a plate of heavily buttered toast and marmalade down on the littered table and, just as I motioned to spark up, she did a 'Paul Daniels' with the ashtray.

'You shouldn't be smokin' in the kitchen, Derry; makes the place stink of 'em,' lectured Mum.

'It's a good job you don't work in the Crown. The punters would blackball yeh.'

'I could work anywhere, son. I'd soon get that dump runnin' shipshape.'

'Trust me, you'd skint Gerry in a week.'

'That fella go skint! Have yeh seen the size of his plot o' land in Stewartstown? He'd make the Duke of Westminster look a pauper.'

'What about Noeleen. How did 'e meet up with her?'

'Ah, Noeleen; now there's a dacent spud. She did a terrible lot for Gerry's mother, Derry. Nursed her for years, God rest her. That woman should've been in a hospice, son, she was very ill. The cancer spread – terror. Noeleen took her in but.'

'Gerry's an OK bloke, Mum,' I remarked.

'Money's his god, Derry. I don't think I've ever seen that

man at Mass, yet,' which gave you nil points on my mother's scorecard.

'The world's changing, Mum. You've got to let people do what they have to do. This isn't 1950s Ireland – this is London in the Nineties, and it's a fuckin' rat race. You don't have time to talk to people, much less help 'em.'

'Don't swear at me, Derry.'

'I'm not swearin' at yeh, I'm explaining. No-one goes to church any more. They don't care about anyone outside their own trivial four walls; it's every man for 'imself. And if yeh see a neighbour drowning, yeh walk on by smiling to yourself – thinkin', *I'm glad I ain't in that sucker's position.*'

'That's not you talking, Derry. It doesn't matter where you are, fella – or how others are behavin'. You treat people with courtesy and respect; you help them if you can. Don't set your sights so low, son.'

'You and you alone, Mum... you and you alone,' the ashtray reappeared from her apron, as she left me to smoke in peace. The mood of serenity in the kitchen was short-lived.

'Derry, drop us at college, sweetheart,' Siobhan snatched a slice of toast and took a drag from my resting cigarette.

'Siobhan, do me a favour; don't ask me for any favours – your credit's shit.'

Siobhan kissed me on the temple: 'You're my boy, bruv. Giv' us a second to clean me boots.'

Carmel whisked into the kitchen, providing an action replay of Siobhan – another slice of toast went AWOL, another puff on my ciggy was stolen, this time leaving a ruby-ring around the butt.

'What's this I'm hearing about you and Liz O'Grady?' demanded Carmel.

'What's what?' I played dumb.

'Are yeh seein' her?' she pressed.

'What yeh talkin' about?' and dumber.

'Are YOU – goin' OUT – *with* HER? You was spotted canoodlin' with her in the club.'

'What's canoodlin'?'

'She means – you was seen being *very* friendly to *Ms* O'Grady,' chipped in Siobhan.

'I'm always friendly to the citizens of my parish. Why d'yeh think they call me *Derry Friendly?*'

'What's this, Derry – you're goin' with Liz O'Grady?' Mum's prospective-daughter-in-law antenna was activated.

'She came swimmin' with me an' Luke on Sunday, that's all,' I said, knowing that the interrogation was about to move into overdrive.

'Why?' asked Mum.

'I asked her.'

'But, why would yeh do that?' Mum seemed amazed.

'We was talkin', and she said she could do with some exercise. Simple.'

Carmel and Siobhan's laughter was uncontrollable.

'Did she get her *exercise,* then, Derry?' chortled Siobhan.

'You're gettin' a bus, *sweetheart!*' I advised her.

'Ah, c'mon, I'm only teasin' yeh,' pleaded Siobhan. 'Don't be so touchy.'

You could almost hear the machinery in her brain rattling, sifting through the data, to find which indelicate question would elicit the maximal gen on Liz and I. Mum was not well-known for her subtlety.

'I don't understand this, Derry. Luke never mentioned to me that Liz O'Grady went with youse – did yeh tell 'im not to tell me?' is exactly what I told him.

'Don't be daft. You know Luke; he'll prob'ly tell yeh in two weeks' time.'

'She's a good-lookin' woman, Derry. Is this serious? It must be if you're trying to hide it from *me*.'

'What's there to hide? We done a few lengths of doggy-paddle down the baths together.'

'..And you was at the club with her?'

'Sunday. We shared an hour or two.'

'It's definitely serious, Mum. Look at 'im, he's scratchin' the table with his fingernails like an embarrassed little school boy,' noticed Carmel.

'Look, Carmel; just 'cause you and Calan are Love's New Dream, it doesn't mean the rest of us are so desperate for Cupid's arro' to smack us between the eyes. I prefer to see a bit of Life. Know what I mean?'

'Derry, I'm tickled for yeh. Liz is a stunnin' girl and, d'yeh know, incredibly for you, she's intelligent. That means if you reproduced, the baby would at least get half-a-brain!'

'To think I was pesterin' Gerry to give you a job in the Crown. I must be fuckin' mad,' Mum evacuated the kitchen in disgust at my word selection.

'Gerry? What did he say?' Carmel suddenly showed interest.

'Go an' see 'im tonight. If yeh wanna do some sessions, he'll fix you up,' I continued flicking through the sports pages of the Express.

'How much does he pay, Derry?'

'Not sure,' I said shaking my head. 'Six or seven quid; what d'yeh get at Finnegan's?'

'How much do *you* earn?' she asked back.

'Piss-off. Who d'yeh think you are, the Revenue?'

'*Precisely*, Derry. Mind your own business; I'll go an' see him after I get finished tonight,' declared Carmel.

'Derry, can we go? I've got an exam today; I need to be early,' said Siobhan.

'Exam? What, for cuttin' hair?'

'Of course. We 'ave to do loads of 'em.'

'Yeah, okay. Let me finish this fag.'

Luke appeared in the kitchen in his crumpled pyjamas, looking dishevelled, and adroitly spinning a yo-yo horizontally inches from my face.

'Are yeh havin' breakfast, Luke?' asked Carmel.

'Nah... I don't think so. What is there?' Luke asked as I snatched his yo-yo just before it shattered the bridge of my nose.

'Right, that's confiscated. Sit down and eat ya branflakes,' I said assertively.

'I don't want branflakes, they taste rotten,' said Luke pulling a face of horror.

'They're meant to taste rotten; that's how you can tell they're good for you.'

'You haven't got to have branflakes, Luke. We've got Golden Puffs, Boulders..' before Carmel could finish listing the choices available, Luke butt in.

'They're ASDA's-own brands. I don't like 'em; they're not proper.'

'They taste the same, Luke,' said Carmel lacking conviction.

'They don't. Only poor people eat them; that's why they're cheaper,' reasoned Luke.

'Well, that's all there is,' Carmel's patience had eroded.

'I'll have branflakes, then,' said Luke contrarily.

'Awkward bastard.'

* * * * * * *

After dropping Siobhan at her college in Sturry Road, East Ham, I then doubled back to Seven Kings to pick up Cliff. He lived with his mother in Chapel Street, about half-a-mile from our house. Both of his elder brothers had fled the nest and married, and both were now divorced. He told me that he'd no memory of his father, visual or otherwise – he died from TB when Cliff was four years old. His dad hailed from the west coast of Ireland, Cleggan, close to Connemara. But his mum was a born-and-bred Cockney from Bethnal Green. The only time that Cliff had visited Ireland, was when he accompanied me on one of my regular jaunts to the Six Counties last year. He felt no compulsion to explore his father's roots and homeland. He remained half-Irish in blood only. A refreshing change from the plastic Paddy 'syndrome', I suppose.

Cliff opened the passenger door with car-thief deftness: lift the door a centimetre, pull it out a centimetre, then lower it an inch, thereby expediting a smooth entry.

'When are yeh gonna get this piece of junk sorted, Derry?' asked Cliff.

'This piece of junk's helpin' to pay your wages, bruvver,' I reminded him.

'True, it's embarrassin', though; watchin' you roll up in a reject from *Mad Max Beyond Thunderdome* – I've got neighbours, Derry!'

'Screw 'em.'

'Where's today's first port of call? Stop in for the *cure* at the Crown?'

'Don't even joke, Cliff. The rest of this week – No, make that month, it's goin' to be: Business, Business, Business.'

'Who's the first target?'

'Target? We're not 'soldiers' in the Cosa Nostra; we're collectin' banknotes from people who can scarcely afford to feed themselves.'

'That's correct; and so far, you're five-'undred quid down.'

'Try replacing the term 'you' with *we*.'

'*We* are five-'undred quid down. Better?' I nodded my approval.

'We'll 'ave to pick up yesterday's run later,' I stretched over and lifted Eamon's ledger off the back seat.

'Now, then, let's see: Iona Weaver, Cobbold Street.'

'That runs down the side of the bingo hall, Derry.'

'Yeah, I know. Number 38; she rents the whole 'ouse.'

'D'yeh want to fill-up with some grease first?' Cliff asked eagerly.

'Does yer mammy not feed you enough already? Look at the size of yeh, yeh fat bastard.'

'It's this cold weather; makes me feel hungry all the time. There's a cafe on the corner of Victoria Road, it's well-mad. Big, fuck-off oval plates – real pukka tucka.'

'We'll call in there after we've seen Mrs Weaver,' I relented.

'Cool.'

There was just enough frost covering the lids on the black wheelie bins to scoop-up a snowball. The bracing, cold air was sufficiently extreme to leave Cobbold Street deserted. Cliff was struggling to fit his hands into a pair of thermal gloves before removing himself from the car. The majority of the houses were enriched by a combination of pebbledashing and painted brickwork. Almost all had new windows – No.38 was an exception. The rotting, wooden window-frames and the dog shit, which virtually formed a top-layer over the lawn, gave clear indication of a rented property and, a negligent landlord, whose expenditure on maintenance and repair was lamentable.

A friendless roller skate and a three-wheeled doll's pram

lent clutter to the path, along with two refuse sacks full of old clothes.

'What's she payin' for this gaff, Derry?'

'Six-fifty.'

A 1970s *Smile* sticker stuck in the corner of the front window represented the only patent form of decoration.

Cliff pressed the doorbell. Silence. I pushed my face against the dusty window – and, although only net curtains were hanging, I was unable to make out any clear images.

'I bet she's hidin' behind the sofa,' said Cliff talking from experience .

'I dunno . Something's not right in there.'

The letter-box flap wouldn't open, and my initial feeling was that it had been blocked up to repel unwelcome mail – or debt collectors.

'She's playin' games with us, Derry. Let's kick the door in.' No sooner had Cliff proposed this direct line of action, than I had began to do exactly that.

'You fuckin' mad bastard; I didn't mean *kick the door down!'*

'I think there's a fire.'

'What?'

'FIRE! You know, burning timber – burning flesh,' with that, Cliff gave the door a fierce, karate-style kick just above the lock. That was the door open. But something behind the door was preventing it from opening fully. I forced my wiry frame through the gap. A woman's body was slumped on the floor in a foetal position cradling a baby in her arms.

Listless eyes – the woman's face was turning blue, and there was no hint of life from the baby, either. Smoke was beginning to fall down the stairs. The woman had a deep gash on her face which appeared to run from ear to mouth, but there was so much blood on her face and around the cut it was difficult to be certain. The baby's face was unmarked.

'They must of fell down the stairs, Derry. Look at the poor cow, she's still holdin' onto the baby. What the fuck d'we do?'

'Get up the stairs, Cliff. Check every room. MOVE!'

'How 'bout these two? You'll 'ave to give 'em the kiss of life or something.'

'I would if I knew how to, but I don't.' This wasn't entirely true. I had attended a two-hour, first-aid crash course at Kinneret, a kibbutz in Tiberias, down by the Sea of Galilee. But that was nine years ago, and I was suffering badly from a Gold Star (kosher beer) hangover and was hardly listening, much less absorbing the life-saving knowledge being bestowed by the Spanish kibbutznik, Miguel, who was in charge of the class.

Cliff had vanished, and was yelling and banging doors upstairs.

'I've got two kids up 'ere, Derry. They're not fuckin' breathin',' Cliff's voice was now reduced to a crying wail.

Flashing through my head was the previous night's party on the kibbutz, held in the Volunteers' clubhouse (a subsiding wooden shack which stank of stale beer and tobacco), and the blood-poisoning punch concocted by the girls working in the kitchen – made from untold bottles of brandy, lemon vodka, vermouth, and a large jug of orange cordial. Also fresh in the memory, was a comely Finnish girl, built like Stuart Pearce from the waist down, with whom I'd spent the night. Unfortunately, though, there was scant recollection of Miguel's methodical instruction on 'How to save a fading human spirit'.

A single wire of blood trickled down the side of the woman's mouth – I was now convinced that the woman I presumed to be Mrs Weaver, was dead. My mind was made up –

the baby would derive most benefit from the limited medical care I was able to offer.

Lifting both mother and baby together, I nudged the door wide open with my boot. Blood from the cut on Mrs Weaver's face was dripping onto the baby, and made for a grisly sight as I laid their limp bodies down on my coat, which I had spread over the hard, frozen path. Smoke was billowing out into the street but, inexplicably, the residents of Cobbold Street continued to be blind to the horror and drama unfolding at No.38.

'This is unreal. Where is everyone for Chrissake? If we'd been parking across somebody's drive they'd be firin' a letter off to their MP by now,' said Cliff, as he cleared a space on the path for two children whose faces were blackened by smoke: a boy, who was maybe six years old, and a sweet, serene-looking girl, perhaps a year younger. The boy was breathing weakly – his sister was likely dead.

Cliff had composed himself and was dealing with the emergency services via his mobile phone, which mercifully had a clear line.

'Undo the buttons round their necks, Cliff,' I advised, as I prepared to resuscitate the baby. To me, he (could of been a girl for all I knew) looked tiny, less than a month old was my guess.

One key step in the mouth-to-mouth procedure that I could recall, was to tilt back the 'patient's' head and to lift the jaw, so to move the tongue as far as is possible from the back of the throat. If cyanosis takes place, the lack of oxygen in the blood would cause damage to the brain within a few minutes. Also, I was aware that with infants, you should seal your lips over their mouth *and* nose when blowing your breath into them.

I had never held a baby so small and was wary of crushing bones – and, consequently, inflicting further injury on the ill-fated tot. Delicately lifting the elfish bundle, I drew a deep breath and commenced a series of gentle puffs. Cliff studied my every move intently, as he psyched himself up in readiness to mimic my technique and, God-willing, revive the girl he'd rescued from upstairs in the blazing house.

Although only a minute or so had elapsed since fleeing from the flames, it felt like an age – still no neighbour had ventured forth to aid our clumsy stab at playing the 'hero'. Far more likely to induce a panic attack, though, was the conspicuous absence of a howling siren, to alleviate the pressure building up on this nightmarish, winter's morning.

The movement of the baby's chest was slight, but it was an uncontestable indication of life. I continued to breathe for the 'wee' boy, then, holding him like a rugby ball, darted over to the other side of the street to 'bash the grannie' out of each door until a reply was found: the startled occupant opened the door and, before she near-fainted, the baby was thrust into her arms.

'Take care of him, love – ambulance is on its way,' the grey-haired lady hadn't time to recover from her shock, or to utter a word; I was back with the remaining casualties in a split second.

The girl that Cliff had taken responsibility for, looked to be experiencing a dramatic upsurge in fortune. Now breathing independently, a healthier colour was flooding into her cheeks. Cliff was overjoyed.

'She's alive, Derry; she's *alive,*' he yelled.

'You're doin' brilliant, Cliff. Keep the boy warm – cuddle 'im. Where's that fuckin' ambulance?'

As the heat from the house warmed the ground around us, finally a crowd gathered, some of them, simply out of a ghoulish fascination to witness first-hand dolour and terror. Others tried to help: one lady knelt down beside the girl, another next to the boy, whom Cliff had actually succeeded in coaxing a few words from.

Belatedly I turned my attention to the children's mother. I fleetingly contemplated their future, and, what shape and quality it would have, should their mum not survive. How much gratitude, if any, would they feel towards Cliff and I for preserving *their* lives?

Pinching her nostrils closed, I blew frantically into her mouth; repeating the procedure four times. I pressed lightly on her neck with two shaking, claret fingers but the carotid artery failed to provide a pulse. Cardiac arrest, essentially, means the heart has closed down and no longer wishes to pump blood around the body – this is very bad. Solution? I didn't have one. Sure, there's been many a time I've watched Hawkeye perform 'miracles' in *M*A*S*H,* by squashing guts back into bodies and bandaging them back up again but, this wasn't Vietnam – or Hollywood. External Chest Compression was not my forte, however, no-one else stepped forward to offer their services, so I placed one hand on her chest, put the other hand on top and interlocked my fingers. I wasn't confident enough to depress her chest too forcefully – 20 compressions failed to ignite a spark of activity in the heart. For the first time I was worried that I'd 'messed up', and caused even greater damage.

While not panicking, I felt deflated and slumped back on my knees to look up at the heavens. There was no face up there looking back at me, though; accordingly, I fell back on my, as of now, speciality, 'the Kiss of Life'. I wearily dragged the sleeve of my jumper across my brow; despite the icy weather conditions I was sweating profusely. I'd become so engrossed with the situation, that the arrival of the ambulance had escaped my notice. Two strong arms joined up at my waist and raised me to a standing position.

'Have a break, son; I'll take over now,' the professionals were in charge.

'Do we know this lady's christian name?' asked the ambulance driver.

'Iona – Iona Weaver,' advanced a voice from the crowd. 'She's got four children,' added another neighbour who, rather enthusiastically, forced her way to the front of the throng jostling for the best view.

'*Four* children!' I screamed, 'we only got three out of the house; two kids and a baby.'

Cliff grabbed at the female paramedic's shoulder: 'We checked ev'ry room; I'm sure we did.'

'Don't worry, sir. They could be at school, or staying with family – at a friend's house,' a comforting thought, but she moved straight over to the fireman in charge and relayed the news of the fourth child.

The man who lifted me up was bent over Mrs Weaver, with his heavy hands bearing down on her chest, ready to pound into her sternum – having done this, he rapidly adjusted his body to continue inflating her lungs.

Flashing blue lights illuminated the overcast sky. The full battery of support vehicles and troops were at hand: the fire brigade, police, and a second ambulance team moved slickly about their business. I escorted the back-up ambulance crew over to the house where I'd left the baby. 'How is he?' asked one.

'I gave him mouth to mouth, got a pulse; he was breathing.'

'Well done. You must of had good training,' I smiled politely and mumbled, 'Yeah, quality.'

I trudged back to where Mrs Weaver laid. Cliff met me – placing his hands on my jaw, he pushed my head up.

'You okay, Derry?' I didn't answer. 'Yeah, everything's gonna be alright, Derry,' Cliff carried the conversation solo: 'Look out, mate, here come the Filth; prob'ly try an' stick the fire on us – wankers,' said Cliff covering his mouth.

A thought struck me – it was the middle of December but there was no festive decorations in Mrs Weaver's house.

'There wasn't a Christmas tree in the house; no tinsel or Christmas cards... nothing,' I said to the officer. The intonation of his speech was calm and soothing: 'Perhaps she wasn't planning to be around to celebrate it,' he said ominously.

'You don't think she'd torch the house herself; burn her own kids?'

'At this stage, sir, we couldn't say. What was your relationship with her?'

'Relationship? I've never seen her before today,' I answered defensively.

'What was you doing here, then?' he asked with an accusing slant which only the police and tax inspectors' derive pleasure from the use of.

The gravity of the circumstances did not rob me of my innate ability to protect my non-tax-paying, dole-claiming status: 'I was in the area; I was doing a favour for a good friend of mine.'

The PC pulled out his black notebook and flipped open the cover with one hand: 'Who was you doing the favour for?'

'I'm not being funny with yeh, mate, but – can we do this later? I need to know what's happening with these people.'

My focus shifted to the ambulance crew administering medical care to Mrs Weaver. Who was this woman? If this was her life 'done and dusted', what a way to go. An austere stranger – me, fumbling about her corpse doing bodge repairs. Game over, no dignity.

* * * * * * *

My intention to hide away in the Crown with just a Guinness and a roll-up for company, was only partially successful. I couldn't block Iona Weaver's face out of my thoughts. Irish women are very beautiful. Iona Weaver was very beautiful. I'd slipped away from Cobbold Street at the earliest opportunity. My aim was to go to the hospital but I wasn't up to it. Luke was used as an excuse to exit the bleak aftermath – and I needed it. I told them that I was the only one able to make Luke take his medicine, then drove off leaving Cliff to mop up. Confirmation of her death hadn't been made at the scene, and when I telephoned the hospital from the Crown, they were unwilling to tell me anything. I didn't really need telling.

Noeleen sat down by my side and planted a pint on the table.

'Well, Derry, have you any news?'

'The only news I have, Noeleen, is bad. Dad always says "Every day's a bonus: live while you can, and die when you can't help it". He's right.'

'You look dreadful, Derry. What's wrong?'

'I'm great. There's nothing wrong with me.'

'Yer clothes are all dirty – you stink!' Noeleen fanned away the smoky reek with her hands.

'Cheers! I don't think much of your chat-up lines. I've come straight from work; giv'us a break.'

'No problem, Derry. I was just checkin'; as long as yeh scrub up before takin' Liz out tonight.'

'*Am I* taking Liz out tonight?'

'Sure, have yeh lost interest in the girl already, Derry?'

'You're right, I forgot. Sorry, bad day at the office. Is Liz upstairs?'

'She's away visitin' an ol' school friend. Brona Kennedy, she's living up in Harlseden. Are you okay, Derry – what's the bad news?'

'Bad news?'

'You said the only news you had was bad.'

'We were supposed to be working on a house in Cobbold Street. I walked into a fire,' I took a mouthful of stout.

'A fire – GOD! Was anyone hurt, Derry?' gasped Noeleen.

'I'm waiting to hear,' Noeleen spotted blood on my sleeve and gripped my hand.

'Who was in there, Derry?'

'A young mum and her kids... they were all in a bad state. I'm worried,' an understatement.

'Have *you* been to the hospital?' said Noeleen trying to spy where the blood had leaked from.

'I've no injuries. Just shock. I left Cliff talking with the police – he'll be at the hospital.'

'Would yeh like me to run you up there, Derry; St. David's is it?'

'Yeah. I'll go later. You better cancel with Liz for me.'

'I will. What d'yeh call this woman, Derry, would I know her?'

'Iona Weaver,' I paused to look up at a collage of 'Irish' pubs on a poster above Noeleen's head. In the middle was Tynan's Bridge House Bar. All I desired in the whole world was to be whisked off to this nondescript hostelry, indulging in drink, and messin' with a tight cell of real hard boyos, dissecting the day's racing and hurling. I had no idea where in Ireland this bar was, but I wanted to be there – devoid of any connection or knowledge of the fire.

'Weaver,' considered Noeleen. 'What age would she be?'

'She's no age, Noeleen – she's a child herself. How the hell she could manage four kids, I don't know,' Gerry drifted over to our table armed with a paintbrush and a tin ice-bucket.

'How's you, Derry?' he asked.

'Rockin',' Gerry dusted down the ashtray with his brush and gave Noeleen a 'look'. Sharp as a Stanley blade, Gerry was alert to an *atmosphere*.

'Just booked a local lad, Derry. Padraig Fallon; a singer/song-writer. Dungannon boy,' said Gerry.

'Is he any good?' I asked.

'Doubt it. He's cheap but. He'll be playin' this Saturday an' Sunday. Make a change from the karaoke if nothing else.' The last singer Gerry hired went down like a fortune-teller on the RMS *Titanic*. Julie Evangelista, she called herself. A risible vocal talent was twinned with a Les Dawsonesque ability on the ivories. The 'gig' was brought to a premature end, when she burst into tears and legged it, after receiving an unyielding stream of unsavoury abuse that Eddie Izzard would of wilted under – 'She makes Bonnie Langford sound like a diva,' quipped Tony Button, the Crown's resident critique. 'Flip, that girl must know a lot of songs,' hollered Paddy Meegan. 'For she won't get off the fuckin' stage!'

'Will I take you home, Derry?' offered Noeleen.

'I'll have a pint first, Noeleen. Thanks.' While she told Gerry of the day's events, my eyes bored into the grooves carved on the table by browned off drinkers as if they were of spellbinding interest.

'What will we ever do with you, Derry Sheehan,' lamented Gerry. Though it was seldom evident by his manner, Gerry was fond of me.

'A question I ask regularly, too, mate,' I sighed. A mobile phone tintinnabulated the William Tell overture.

'We've got to ban these phones, Noeleen. They should have

no place in here,' said Gerry.

'It's like a disease, Gerry. They can't help themselves,' I said, as the three of us looked around the pub at the dozen or so prats with mobiles glued to their lugs.

'You'd think they'd want to escape from the City when they come in here – not drag it in with 'em,' said Noeleen.

'Every one of them's talkin' shit. I guarantee it.'

'I'm surprised yeh don't carry one yourself, Derry, what with this new high-level job yeh have.'

'I'm one of the old school, Gerry. I prefer the personal touch; face-to-face. There's no confusion that way.'

'Good man,' said Gerry.

5. STEP INSIDE LOVE

'Oh, you're right there, says yer man. We'd like to do a piece on the local hero – the Country should know what this brave young man did today,' Geraldine emptied a tray of mugs into the bowl of suds, as she told Mum about her brush with a scribe from the national press.

'He was nearly after wrestling me to the ground to get by, Corien. Persistent little frigger but; says that they want Derry to be on their front page.'

'Was he offerin' money, Geraldine?' asked Mum.

'He was indeed; promised his life away.'

The minute Geraldine heard news of the fire, she came round to proffer her moral support and, more importantly, her culinary expertise: enough salad sandwiches were produced to feed the season-ticket holders of Barcelona Football Club. Also in tow were Seán, Sheila and Daragh. Everyone was crammed into the kitchen, bar Luke and Sean, who seemingly sat captivated by Charlie Dimmock's green fingers in the telly-room.

Daragh was tugging at Geraldine's jeans. 'What are yeh lookin', cub?' Daragh pointed to the Irish-born pine table which had made the ferry-journey with us twenty-plus years back. On it was presented an ambrosian selection of grub.

'I could eat two of them pies, Mummy,' whispered a bright-eyed Daragh, showing little sign of tiredness, despite the late hour. The fruit-pies Daragh hungered after, were of the butter-fly winged – apple and blackcurrant variety.

'Fish fingers, fruit-pies and Skips, are all that wee gyp'll touch,' said Geraldine handing over *one* fruit pie to Daragh.

'I've just had Liz O'Grady on the phone, Geri. She's worried sick about our Derry.'

'I heard they were together, Corien. Derry smitten, is he?'

'Thinks she's the greatest thing since penicillin. Won't tell me anything of course,' complained Mum.

'Your Derry never tells anyone anything. The boy's very deep, Corien. But how could you fault him? What he did, savin' those children – and their mummy; unbelievable.'

'I know, I'm very proud of him. I'd like to see him settled, though, Geraldine. He spends too much of his time dodgin' about. Eamon Mooney's been on the phone five times tonight. Tell me, what's he doin' mixed up with the likes of him? Look at your Kathleen; goin' to university – it's brilliant. She's got a purpose. So confident.'

'They're all different. Could you imagine Derry at university? He'd cause friggin' mayhem!'

'You're right. He wouldn't have a chance to unpack his case; takes a dislike to people for no reason. He's deadly but.'

'Is he sleeping, Corien?'

'He's havin' a bath. The shock's hit him like a supermarket shoppin' bill. He can't believe the Weaver woman's still alive; asked me to order a wreath when he come in.'

'Do they know what started the fire?'

'They haven't said. The police left just before you arrived. They asked Derry a load of questions. A detective congratulated him for all he did.'

'Still managed to leave me feeling as guilty as Jack the Ripper, though.'

'Derry! Come here – let me give you a hug,' gushed Geraldine.

'The phone hasn't stopped since you went up, Derry: Liz,

Cliff twice... and Eamon Mooney every 15-minutes,' said Mum.

'Mr Popular today, aren't I!'

'You're not goin' out, Derry?'

'I need to go and see Eamon.'

'What about?'

'He's got a bit of work for me and Cliff.'

'What happened to this full-time job you had lined up?'

'It's in the pipeline. Don't worry, Mum,' I reassured her.

'When you've had children of your own, you'll understand what *worry* is.'

'I want to get some cash organised for Christmas. I'm in between careers at the moment.'

'What is it you wanna be, Derry?' asked Geraldine.

'I wanna make tea at the BBC,' tonight, *Matthew*, I'm going to be Joe Strummer.

'You were always very ambitious, Derry,' Geraldine said drily.

'You'll be wantin' to get Liz a special Christmas present, I suppose,' reasoned Mum.

'Absolutely, a nice velvet frock!'

I grabbed a handful of quarter-cut salad sandwiches, slurped down a strong tea and said farewell.

'Don't wait up, people.'

'Peace be with you, Derry,' said Geraldine.

Know your limitations and prioritise, said Eamon at our last meeting. Good advice, amigo. I made a B-line over to the Crown. There's no time to take stock or wind down. Worries about work, sex, alcohol, cloud my vision: I have got to get a grip. The fire has enforced a break from routine, but even that's not enough to prevent a series of maudlin daydreams.

My planned flying visit, to arrange a rendezvous with Liz

after work, was thwarted when Lance Friel noticed my arrival. Chiefly identifiable by his love of the primary colours, with his ill-fitting puffa jackets, combined with a fervent narcissism, he was the last person I wished to bump into.

'Move to the groove; swing with the strings; *race to the bass!'* Lance was doing a shadow-boxing-type of dance to the Four Tops' 'It's The Same Old Song'.

Dispensing with his junior school level of word-rhyming, Lance proceeded with an affected West Indian patois.

'Derry, my man. Gimme some skin!' Lance presented me with his hand for a slap, which I pointedly ignored.

Third or fourth generation Irish, Lance had a delusion he was in possession of Blackman cool. He tried to promote (unsuccessfully) the self-styled nickname 'Bunny', à la Paul Ince's lame adoption of 'the Guv'nor' title at Manchester United. Like all the other poor fools with goatee beards, he grew it with the singular intention of adding some depth to his hollow personality, but all it did was make him look a twat. He was never in the company of a mate(s). However, he did pounce on each and every customer as they entered the pub – or went to the toilet, delivering the same, well-rehearsed, clichéd responses before offering to buy them a drink; apart from the skint and stotious, most declined.

Ever alert to the 'comings and goings' in the bar, Liz was alive to my plight.

'Derry, can I see you for a second?'

'Yeah, sure. Catch yeh later, Lance.'

'Safe, man. Safe.'

Liz had the kind of figure that could make a pair of beige Marks & Spencer slacks and a cheesecloth shirt look sexy. She was wearing an altogether more desirable and classic outfit tonight, though, in the shape of a low-slung vest and stonewashed 501's.

Steering me to a less crowded area, I felt a sense of foreboding and a distinctly negative vibe. Was she going to give me the Spanish Archer – El Bow? We sat down at a table awash with empty glasses and an overflowing ashtray. I braced myself for the worst. What she did next left me red-faced and open to the sort of ridicule and insults reserved only for the very weakest specimens of pub-subculture. Liz leaned across the table and planted a lingering, sensual kiss which embodied so much passion and verve, I almost passed out. Friends that I'd socialised with since the tender age of fifteen bore witness to the most momentous and pivotal few seconds of my short life.

The 'kiss' was something that I had been praying for since the day I first clapped eyes on Liz. Now that it had actually taken place, I wasn't ready for it. There was no agonising build up or body language involved, just, Bang! Once the cheering and jeering had died down, I endeavoured to compose a laid-back front, like it was no big deal. Stunned into silence, eventually I blurted out, 'Thank you!'.

'Well. *Thank you*, Derry!'

'What did I do to deserve that?'

'Did I embarrass you, you're lookin' a bit scarlet?'

'Not embarrassed, I wasn't expecting it.'

'I spoke to your mum on the phone, Derry. When I heard about the fire, yeh know, I was upset. Didn't want to lose you; I've hardly got to know you,' Liz sounded deadly earnest.

'You don't get rid of me that easy. I'm indestructible, Teflon coated!'

'That's reassuring. It was a wonderful thing you did today. Your mum said the family are goin' to be alright.'

'Thank God.'

'I thought you wasn't religious?'

'Don't start!'

'Are yeh havin' a drink?'

'Nah. I've got to dash in a minute, see some people.'

'Sounds very mysterious.'

'Just work. Can I see you later?'

'You certainly can,' Liz's eyes locked into mine and welcomed me in.

'Sorry about tonight. I wanted to take you somewhere nice. Go for a meal or something.'

'Don't be silly. Will you be back before closin'? I said I'd work after you cancelled.'

'Definitely. I won't be long,' damned straight.

'Are you sure you feel okay, Derry?'

'Fine. Why, do I look rough?'

'I didn't mean it like that. The shock of it all must be hard to deal with?'

'We had other things to do, today, Liz. It was a change in plans that made us go there. I keep thinking; what if?'

'I know it's easy for me to say, but that's fate. It's everyone's fate. When yer luck's in..'

'That simple?'

'Well, I'm not sayin' I'd make the world's greatest post-traumatic stress counsellor.'

'You're not doin' too bad,' Liz put a playful fist into my face.

'I've really got to go, Liz – be back as soon as I can.'

'I'll be waitin'.'

* * * * * * *

I knew Eamon would be in a cold sweat over the report by the

Fire Investigation Team. If they established the fire was caused by unsafe electrics, he'd be up Shit Creek minus his paddle.

Even if he displayed a Lilliputian degree of humanity or concern for the Weaver family, it would of been something. But that wasn't Eamon's way, first and foremost was self-preservation. Immediately he got wind of the news, Eamon was desperate to visit me at home. That was never an option, as he was roundly demonised in the Sheehan quarter of Burnley Road. My parents' negative opinion of Eamon was universally shared within their confined circle of friends: he was a leech, feeding from the poor, and exploiting their misfortune and poverty.

On first look, it wasn't an inaccurate judgement to make. For my part, I had seen and, benefited, from a side of Eamon's nature, albeit rarely shown, which was altogether more endearing. Plus, Eamon was different... he knew how to make money. This I respected.

To avoid the hassle of a third party complicating matters, we arranged to meet on neutral ground. Eamon had a yacht moored at Limehouse Basin, off the Commercial Road, beside the Rotherhithe Tunnel. Not exactly Monte Carlo in the summer, it was desolate in December. The section of Commercial Road adjacent to the marina, was uniquely favoured with a profusion of exhaust-fume tainted Chinese restaurants. In spite of the squalor and filth neighbouring the inner-city location, once setting foot on the harbour, it felt as if you had been transported to an anomalous plane.

This was a playground for 'liquid' money men. A few nouveau riche Captain Pugwashes with tacky vessels had wormed their way in to the old Regents Canal Dock, but the majority were serious players. I was waiting for Bob Hoskins aka Harold Shand, to leap off his launch and drag me on board for a glass of beer, before severing my jugular vein with a saw-edged bottle neck. No such luck, though. Eamon came bounding down the gangplank, greeting me like a long-lost brother.

Big hugs and macho handshakes were followed by a startling admission by Eamon: 'I love you, Derry,' I don't think he noticed the guy behind him pushing a Topic wrapper round the harbour with a bristle-less broom. He checked me up and down with a squint in his eyes, wiped a drip off his nose, then proceeded with his sweeping.

'Steady, Boss. That geezer over there thinks we're a pair of irons.'

'That's ol' Donny Saveloy. He's worked here all his life; they was after building the marina around him.'

Eamon welcomed me on to the Ballintober for our clandestine heart-to-heart.

'How the other half live. This is a bit special,' it reminded me of the inside of a gypsy's caravan.

'Have yeh not seen her before, Derry?'

'You've never invited me.'

For 150 years, the Regents Dock was London's principal gateway to England's canal network. Ton after ton of coal entered through the Limehouse Lock on colliers and was then loaded into barges, and distributed to London's gasworks. You won't find any dockers swinging death-dealing hooks now, though. Today it's all river-view apartments and sailing boats. What a waste of water.

Eamon filled two heavy crystal tumblers with Jameson whiskey.

'Are you tryin' to get me nicked, I've got to drive home from here?'

'You'll never get pinched, Derry; you're a lucky bastard. That's what I like about yeh.'

'I'd love to own a boat like this, Eamon. You've arrived when you've got a baby like this parked in the marina.'

'If you stick with me, you'll get one – I can depend on you, Derry. It could of been nasty at Iona's if you wasn't there.'

'It *was* nasty,' Eamon pulled down the blinds on the canted rectangular windows.

'How is Iona? I phoned the hospital; they told me nothing. Yer ma said that she was stable,' Eamon worked both hands through his thick red locks and joined them at the back of his head.

'She looked like a stiff to me, Eamon. Frightened the fuckin' life out of me.'

'Me and Iona was very close at one time, Derry,' Eamon gulped down his whiskey.

'I see. Does she have a husband?' I had no interest in Eamon's personal life but Iona roused my intrigue.

'He's away to meet his maker. Gerard, worked as a steel erector. Fell 40ft from a site in Soho – Beak Street, I think it was.'

'Shit, she's had some luck.'

'Tore her apart, son,' Eamon refilled his glass. 'Will I make some grub?'

'You havin' some?' I asked, as I hated being watched eating.

'I am surely. All this stress is killing me. I've not had a scrap all-day.'

Eamon served up a skillet of cordon bleu bacon and eggs. I poked at the bacon with my fork: 'Nice and crispy. It doesn't get any better than this, Eamon.'

'Was there any sign of what started the fire?' Niceties observed, Eamon finally moved on to the crucial point of our nautical natter.

'Cliff thinks it started in the bedroom. Was she a smoker?'

'Does the Pope support Celtic?'

'Maybe it was a ciggy, then?'

'Maybe,' Eamon glanced at me before stabbing his egg.

'The woman next-door was a right ol' pig. I heard her rabbitin' to the cops, slaggin' off Iona – talk about character assassination.'

'She's anti-Irish. Black-hearted bitch, that one.' Eamon tapped me on the knuckle: 'What did the police ask *you*?'

'Usual thing, "Do you want to tell us all about it, son?". Told them I was a friend of yours, come to price up a paintin' job.'

'That's fine, Derry. That's fine.'

'We'll be back to work in the morning. There's a lot of ground to cover in the next couple of days, but it's under control. Will you still be goin' to Ireland at the weekend?'

'I'd like to, Derry. Circumstances being what they are, I may need to stick around.'

'Well, if it's alright with you, I'm gonna bolt. Giv'us a shot of peppermint cordial, Eamon. Last thing I need now is a driving ban.'

'Sure. Appreciate your company, Derry. You've got a lot on your plate right now. But keep in touch. Okay?'

'Don't worry, Eamon. I'm in control.'

We climbed the ladder from the galley and stood on deck. Eamon made me a black coffee to complement my sickly chaser and topped himself up with the 'water of life'.

'Are you sleepin' here tonight?' I asked.

'I will be. Nancy's waitin' for me over there,' Eamon used his glass as a guide, as we looked across the glistening lights bouncing off the still water.

'Not another fuckin' Chinese?'

'Another fuckin' Chinese, is right. Nancy's the worst cook I ever met, Derry,' I returned Eamon's smile and we both laughed.

****

I came away from the yacht with renewed zest and vigour. What 12 hours earlier was shaping up to be the worst day since Middlesbrough relegated Chelsea in a play-off, was unfolding into a pleasingly memorable day.

"The coward does it with a kiss". What was Oscar Wilde on when he wrote that? The most brave and heroic thing I ever did was letting Liz kiss me in the Crown. I couldn't wait to get back. The purgatory of driving down the A13 suddenly became a poetic affair, as previously unseen beauty leapt at me from buildings I ordinarily closed my eyes to. With Dad's Tornados' cassette installed in the tape player, and 'Telstar' ripping holes in my long-suffering tweeters, my metallic blue Alfa Romeo hurtled past Canary Wharf, Billingsgate fish market, McDonald's – even the Woolwich ski slope furnished my head with a romantic vision. Life *is* sweet.

****

'You've been a massive drinker, Patrick. What did you expect with your health?'

Pat Dawe was stunned by his doctor's frank prognosis: 'Quit the booze – or start looking for a nice plot down the cemetery.'

Dr. Warren Brennan was no stranger to the evils of drink himself, so when he gave you the last rites, you had to listen. The conversation between Pat and Ciaran White, was taking place in the immaculately kept 'Gents' in the Crown. Pristine, gleaming tiles provided an appropriately clinical background for Pat's emotional and groggy ramble.

With one hand flat against the wall in front, Pat was just managing to piss into the sparkling steel urinal without falling in.

'I worked hard all my life, Ciaran. The kids never went short. Josie's never strayed. I don't fuckin' deserve this,' cried Pat.

'You're not dying from cancer, Pat. Quit the booze; he's only told you to quit the booze,' Pat's head swung to the left. '*Only*, the boy says, Derry.'

'If you cut down, it would be a start,' said Ciaran,

'CUT DOWN... I can't believe he's doin' this to me,' Pat's bitterness was switched to the Almighty.

'Try takin' a half to begin with, Pat,' I suggested.

'A half-pint! Fuck that for a tin o' crackers,' said Ciaran zipping up. 'Derry, could I have a word in private?'

'Sure,' we left Pat peeing the smelly lemon cubes and bits of chewing-gum to the end of the channel.

We re-convened outside the pub. I assumed that Ciaran wished to seek my advice on some interior design. Wrong.

'I need a bit of cash, Derry. A grand.'

'They have banks now, Ciaran.'

'A bank's no use to me. I heard that you're in charge of finance with Eamon.'

'Who told you that?'

'Cliff. Said you're the man to see.'

'Cliff's got a big mouth. Eamon's the last person you want to be borrowin' money from. Trust me.' I knew it was only a matter of time before Cliff started bragging.

'It's not like I have a choice, son,' said Ciaran.

'Are things that bad?'

'They will be if I don't lay this bet off.'

'You wanna borrow a grand for a punt? Are you windin' me up?'

'You don't understand, Derry. This horse is goin' to *win*. D'yeh get me?' Ciaran's cigar produced a cloud of smoke, so we both moved back a yard.

'Where's the info come from?' I couldn't resist asking.

'My brother-in-law over in Tipp. He's a millionaire. Made his fortune buyin' and sellin' pubs in London. Once every ten years, yeh get a touch like this, Derry.'

'If this is kosher, Ciaran – I'll get you the cash. I want a grand on it meself. Right?'

'The Ostrich. As of today, he's 12-1.'

A hand was massaging my back – 'Are youse two a pair of Eskimos or what? Could yeh not take a seat inside, Derry?' Ciaran's iron filing pupils were drawn to Liz's stiffening, magnetic nipples.

'Ten minutes, Derry. As soon as Noeleen's cashed up, *I'm free*,' I clicked my fingers in Ciaran's face to divert his stare.

'Whenever you're ready, Liz. Any danger of a pint for me and Ciaran?'

'Make it quick, Derry,' Liz stepped back inside.

'She has a *lovely* wee chassis – are you bangin' her, Derry?'

'Behave, Ciaran. When do you want this money?'

'Tomorrow would be nice.'

'Where will you make the bet?'

'All over. No more than two hundred in a shop,' Ciaran took a puff on his cigar and flicked the ash.

'We'll be playin' a different game if that boy doesn't get past the post first,' I informed Ciaran.

'What game's that, now?'

'Russian roulette – with Mooney loadin' the bullets.'

Save Peter Canavan leading Tyrone to an elusive senior All-Ireland triumph, there could be no more uplifting a sight than Liz dishing the dirt and Guinness to her fawning admirers in the Crown. Not one of them was capable of rattling, or getting the better of her, she cut down and shredded each comment with equal aplomb.

'Domino Dancing' took me back in time. Not that I was a big fan of the Pet Shop Boys. But as I was waiting for Liz to re-line her eyeliner, the song, which held a particularly nostalgic spot in my pop consciousness, awakened memories of Gran Canaria, and a mentally and physically debilitating vacation. I can't explain why, but even a few days abroad felt like a year spent on Mars as far as stories breaking in the newspapers, and records appearing in the charts were concerned. I never heard the song while I was over there, only saw it listed in the top-twenty, in a 200 pesetas copy of *The Sun*. Months later, though, I found it on the jukebox in a poky Brighton pub. I was working down there painting bedsits for a local property tycoon in the summer of '88. He specialised in crumbling sea-side tenements, for sad, lost souls, who were unlikely to revel in the happy 'bucket and spade' picture-postcard portrait of the town.

* * * * * * *

'Mortimer O'Shea was in earlier, Derry. He was telling me about his boy, Niall. His sufferin' from some rare illness; attacks the nervous system. Ten years old, and the poor lad's wheelchair bound.'

'Niall's a great kid – head never drops. Football mad, he's got the bedroom plastered with Celtic posters. He doesn't have much time left. There's not a thing the doctors can do for him,' this news upset Liz deeply.

'Christ, Derry, his daddy never said.'

'Mortimer's a top man. He wanted to take the family back home. The journey would kill Niall.'

'You've got all these grown men, moanin' about the price of a pint...' Liz sat down on her bed.

'It's a *me me me* society, Liz,' here I was in Liz's bedroom, but the last thing 'in the air' was amour. 'The time is now. Tonight, Tomorrow, not forty years' time. All me dad's worried about is gettin' us lot plugged into a pension... ISAs for Godsake. A load of spotty twats in Armani suits pushin' everyone else's dough around.'

'Lookin' after his kids. That's what you do – when you're a parent, that is.'

'A pension, come off it, Liz.'

'So what have you got to offer me, Derry?' Liz put a Dionne Warwick CD on, and 'Do You Know The Way To San José' sent me into a spin, literally.

'Unconditional happiness,' was my trite reply.

'Is that right, boy?'

The window in Liz's bedroom overlooked the railway line. Lacking the extravagance of peace and quiet afforded by double glazing, the dilapidated, loose-fitting frames blocked out little, if any, of the constant shuddering noise made by the passing freight trains.

'I used to like to hear the sound of the trains at night time when I was a kid. I felt safe. Yeh know, the thought that people were still awake; working, speeding across the country, while I was lying in bed. Dark silence, then, far away in the distance, the gentle rumbling starts up,' I reminisced fondly.

'Me, too. I love this room,' Liz handed me a steaming frothy coffee. 'Not that I get a whole lot of sleep like.'

'How long will you stay, Liz – in Seven Kings, I mean?'

'To be truthful, I'm homesick. That doesn't mean to say I'll leave. But I miss the Donegal air, Derry. The smell of cow shit. It's funny how yeh miss that smell when you're away from it.'

'You're right. It's a lovely smell. D'yeh mind if I roll a fag?'

'Be my guest. After the day you've had, how could I deny you?' Liz sat beside me on the bed, and was scrutinising my rolling technique, as I gathered the tobacco on the Rizla.

'Could I try one; rollin' it?'

'Will you smoke it?'

'I might. I will. Giv' us the stuff.'

'Fuckin' hell, Liz! You only get fifty leaves a pack. Cum 'ere,' I took Liz's hands. 'Lay the paper flat on ya leg. You need good fresh tobacco. Waste of time when it's dry.'

'Do you ever take drugs, Derry?'

'Everyday. Anadin Extra, I'm an addict. Fuck drugs, Liz. They're for sad bastards with no spirit,' our fingers rolled the paper in tandem and I brushed the loose tobacco off her lap with the back of my hand.

'There's some wicked craic back home, Derry. I miss Friday nights with the girls. You'd luv 'em but. Every one of 'em's a spacer. We start early – 6. No messin' with the face and hair. Down the town, and straight into the Dive Bar. Then, it's solid alcohol abuse and ragin'; who's zooming who, and all the week's goings-on.'

'Let's go over this Friday, Liz. Have a "lost weekend".'

'Are ya kiddin'?'

'*No*. I'll get Carmel to book the flights in the morning.'

'We can't.'

'Why not?'

'All sorts of reasons. Work; *money*.'

'Liz, we're goin'. Square it with Noeleen. You and me are

gonna be sittin' in the Dive Bar, at *your* table, waitin' for the wreckin' crew. *This* Friday.'

'Will we, Derry?' Liz said excitedly.

'There's nothing more certain,' Liz studied the home-made snout she was holding.

'I don't have any money, Derry. It's too quick.'

'Don't talk soft, Liz. I'm payin'; *we're goin'*,' Liz smiled.

'I'll pay you back – and I mean it, boy. Every penny. Right?'

'If you want. Money's not important. I like to be generous. It's the only virtue I have.' Liz put the cigarette in her mouth.

'Would yeh give me a light, fella?' she cupped her hands around the flame and my fingers, even though there was no draught to blow the match out.

6. RAINTOWN

Picking at a bag of rank, greasy chips from the normally reliable Jolly Kipper, I bumped into Martin and his kid sister.

'Alright, mate. Where yeh heading?'

'I'm takin' Rosie to her dance class. D'yeh want to come along? You can get a cup of tea.'

'A cup of tea?' I looked at Martin in bewilderment.

'Yeah, a cup of tea – in a real mug,' Martin explained, with a bizarre keenness.

'A cup of tea, in a *real* mug. Let's go!'

Deep in the bowels of the terminally-decaying streets of Whitechapel, next to St. Mary's Church, stood the Rianta Club, above which was the church hall. You could draw a direct parallel with the boxing gym situated above the Royal Oak pub in Canning Town. Both were nurturing and developing potential world champions.

In the midst of all this social deprivation, young girls with gazelle-like grace, and calf muscles a professional athlete would inject nandrolone to achieve, were running through their reels and slip jigs, in readiness for the annual invasion of Ireland. The mission: to wrestle a world title from Dublin. A close second to the 'worlds', was securing a place with one of the many dance troupes presently criss-crossing the globe. The US, Canada, Australia and New Zealand – Europe. The growth was phenomenal.

The reflected glory which the mothers of these thoroughbred dancers basked in, was almost tangible. Most of them watched impassively, pretending to be cool or modest of their child's successes in An Coimisiún Feiseanna held up and down the country – but, underneath, the rivalry was acerbic. The girls (and one or two boys) were hammering out their traditional set dances with the power and speed of a pneumatic drill; then, dashed over to Sister Katelin, who was collecting the class fees and selling a tempting assortment of marshmallow twists, and tangy cola-flavoured strips.

Even a gratuitous cynic like me had to admit that this was a positive and rewarding activity.

'Faster! Faster!' was the teacher's rallying command to one of her pencil-slim prodigies.

'This is serious stuff, Martin. I wouldn't fancy being on the wrong end of one of her tongue lashings,' I observed.

'Too right, it's serious. These kids have got a chance thanks to that lady. If Rosie can stick with it, she can forget Tesco's, or being trapped in front of a fuckin' computer screen. She could be tourin' the world, earning big bucks,' enthused Martin.

'I'll drink to that. Where's this tea, then?'

One of the mini-Flatley's skidded on the heel of her 'heavy' shoes, and flew into the Sister's sweet table at Mach 1, shooting Dolly Mixtures under chairs and to every corner of the hall.

'That reminds me, Derry. Didn't you do a bit of dancing? I seem to remember you prancing around in a little kilt when you was in juniors.'

'I could of been somebody, Martin. I could've been a contender. Jimmy said to me, "It's not your night, kid. They're takin' the price on Wilson: you've got to take a fall in the Hornpipe".'

'I'll give yeh fifty notes if you get up and join in the next dance,' Martin challenged.

'Let's see the colour of it,' Martin pulled out his chequebook.

'Is a cheque acceptable?' he asked.

'A cheque! You're 'avin' a jingle. The only thing that bounce more than your kites are Cathy Hurst's thrup'ny bits.'

Martin covered his face. 'Oh, shit. I don't believe this,' he said to himself. 'He's only gonna do it!'

I pounded my Italian ankle boots on the floor to make sure they made an authentic rat-a-tat-tat noise on the sprung timber. Rosie looked on in amazement, as I tapped out TIP DOWN, TIP DOWN, TREBLE 1,2 1,2 – the first intricate steps of The Blackbird.

Kirby Lynch, TCRG, ADCRG and ex-triple world champion, broke off from orchestrating her U/9s in their rehearsal for a display at the Dagenham Town Show.

All the kids in the hall suspended practice en masse, and I became the centre of attention, as Kirby Lynch advanced menacingly towards me, not looking me in the face; my feet and arms were the only thing she was concerned with.

'Sorry.. I didn't mean to disrupt the class..' I wasn't allowed to finish my apology – or stop dancing.

'Don't stop, keep going. TIP DOWN – TREBLE IN-FRONT – TREBLE HOP BACK,' she barked at me. 'Now on the left leg.'

Why do I get involved in such japes? Fifty quid and a laugh, I considered, was abundant reward for the mild humiliation one had to endure. Martin was creasing up; my new classmates were riveted to every ROCK and HOP, as our tutor, still refusing to let me draw a veil over my boyish prank, stapled my arms to my side with her hands.

'Get your trebles in front, not out to the side – and knees together on the toe swizz!!'

'Sorry, Miss,' I begged, 'I've got to take a breather.'

'Very well; you're excused. Don't waste my time again

unless you're serious.' Phew!

'Fare play to yeh, Derry; *that* was fifty notes well spent,' Martin shook my hand and Sister Katelin brought the much appreciated brew over.

'God bless you, Sister,' I wheezed.

Rosie and a trail of pals skipped past with beaming faces. 'I think she wants you to join her gang, Derry.'

'They look like a pretty cool bunch.'

'Any plans for the weekend, mate?' asked Martin.

'Carmel's just booked me and Liz on a flight to Belfast International.'

'You and Liz?'

'Yep.'

'All systems go with youse two, then?'

'Touch wood. Three o'clock Friday; we're away.'

'Good for you. If you've got any sense, you won't come back.'

'That thought had crossed me mind, Martin.'

****

Even without bringing Liz into the equation, flying out of Gatwick on a Friday afternoon, while every other mug became engulfed in the madness of rush hour, sent a mellowing charge of serenity rushing to my brain and relaxed each sinew and muscle instantaneously.

Whether it was by aeroplane, ferry, or catamaran, it made no difference to me. All 49 pilgrimages that I had made to Ireland, were packed with halcyon memories. Fighting Carmel for the top bunk in our cabin on the overnight Liverpool to Belfast crossing, while Dad was sinking Guinness at the bar and Mum was away ticking the numbers off her bingo card in the lounge area; and feeling supercilious, laughing at the land-lubbers puking their supper into handbags, cups and everything other than a toilet. I felt like Sinbad the Sailor as I watched them turn green. Another highlight was rummaging through the bona fide Paddy knick-knacks in the gift shop. It was the same old gear every year – shamrock T-shirts, tin whistles and cuddly leprechauns – but I loved it: I was on my way to *Ireland*. The accents of the crew were alien, thick Scouse, not Irish, but it was far removed from the Cockney patter I was used to in London, so to me, I was in another country the second we had clambered up the narrow, iron stairs from the carloading bay and reached the check-in and restaurant level. The overpowering recollection of this route, however, was the smoky-bacon crisps smell of the Liverpool Dock.

Holyhead to Dún Laoghaire was a different kettle of fish entirely. In comparison, the relatively straightforward (if you ignore the Birmingham bit) drive up the M6 to Merseyside was a breeze. The trip to North Wales was a nightmare. Especially the final furlong; the dreaded A55. Where were the Romans when this tedious, and neverending section of motorists' hell was conceived?

The proverbial one-horse town, Holyhead has about as much interest and appeal to the departing holidaymaker as a wrapped-in-plastic slice of processed cheese would have for a Frenchman. If you miss the ferry (or in the case of Family Sheehan, the rare miracle of arriving six hours early), the port, and town is a neglected, Welsh wasteland. There is nothing to do in Holyhead. One can only pity the people who live in, and call this ghastly locality home. The only plus point is the swift voyage to the Emerald Isle. I always got a slight twinge of pain, though, as we eased away from the barren landscape: the inevitable fact was that we must return to these dank shores and slate-grey skies at some unearthly hour two weeks later.

Because of the mountains of luggage which accompanied every trip we made as a group, flying was rarely a viable option, other than for the unexpected, brief visit for a funeral or, in contrast, the riotous excellence of a wedding weekend. These were always glorious affairs. We got to see our legions of aunts, uncles and cousins in one hit and, naturally, all the adults were slaughtered, which gave us minors free rein to run amuck. Seldom was Dad so lax on discipline.

As soon as I was old enough to travel independently, however, hanging about airports and jumping on planes, was my preferred mode of transport. Crisp-uniformed pilots and catwalk trolley dollies; the smell of *YvesSaintLaurent* perfume and ludicrously expensive sunglasses represented the spurious glamour of the international jet-setter's (okay, I know I was only gliding over the Irish Sea) lifestyle that I loved to indulge in.

* * * * * * *

For two days and nights, Cliff and I embraced the work ethic of a tenacious Trojan; even a seemingly pointless call on Jimmy Wild proved fruitful. A total of £6,800 was harvested and banked. Eamon was satisfied, and grudgingly issued me with a 72-hour pass. I was to be back on duty first thing Monday morning. Liz was given the green light from Noeleen, and Mum had washed, ironed and folded my shirts.

I chucked my case into the boot and drove to Silvertown, where I picked up a big Celtic cross and chain, engraved on the back of the cross was a short inscription: 2 LIZ LOVE D. I was only going to give it to her if things went uncommonly well, though.

The excitement was building and Grizzled skippers were whirring around in the pit of my stomach. The fiftieth return 'home' was to be spent on foreign soil: Donegal. A brand new tribe to meet and a weekend alone with a girl I had, so far, only sparred with. Viewing the sweeping multi-shades of green pastures from a precarious ridge on a Co. Derry hillside was as close as I had been to Donegal before, when we visited Eleanor Walsh, an old friend of Mum's who had bought a busy guesthouse in the windswept resort Portrush.

Liz was making her own way to Gatwick because she had a prior lunch engagement arranged at Dirty Dick's pub (situated opposite Liverpool St. Station) with a mate who was temping for a recruitment agency in Moorgate.

I left my car in a staff space allocated for Abbey Rent-A-Car inside the airport. Ronan Toman was my sidekick in Greece. I met him on a 22-hour boat journey from Piraeus heading for Crete. Ronan was a clubby Dubliner and an unaffectedly funny man. We ended up sharing a room at Gingilos Tavérna in the tiny village Kaló. Two months were whiled away picking olives under the blistering sun for buttons and as much liver-pickling retsina you were able to keep down. I was shocked to see what a fat bastard he'd matured into. The boy was a fitness freak back in the old days.

While I remained comatose clinging to my blanket on the stone floor, Ronan would be out on the balcony sweating with his skipping-rope, swinging it backwards and forwards, and moving like a 5 per cent body-fat middleweight. My head swelled as I cast an eye over his rotund torso; standing proud, because *I* still registered the same 155 pounds on the scales as I did in 1987. The fact that my old buddy was providing me with free parking ensured a limit on the piss-taking, as I nudge

nudge, wink winked him my car keys.

'What about ye, Derry? How's life treating yeh?'

'Sweet as. Family alright?'

'Doin' the best, mate. You'll have to come over one Sunday for dinner and meet the kids. Norah would love to see you.'

'Definitely. I'll give you a call when I get back.' There was a mile-long queue of seriously impatient customers behind me so I made a speedy exit.

'Cheers then, Derry. I'll get yer motor valeted while you're away. Pick her up from the same spot.'

'I owe you one, Ronan. Thanks, mate.' I thought the world of Ronan, he was a cracker. But I wasn't a big fan of 'organised' Sunday dinners. I knew his wife. He met Norah on the beach in Eilat. Love at first sight: Strawberry Blonde, delicious. We parted company soon after. They had me to thank for their joyous union. Israel was not on Ronan's itinerary. I convinced him that it was in his best interest to go and paid his £70 airfare. The flight from Athens to Tel Aviv was memorable. Jon Moss, handsome devil, and drummer with Culture Club, was sat next to us and joined in a carefree, mid-air session. Charming man, very down to earth.

Less charming was our 'welcome' at Ben Gurion airport. We were confronted on the runway by a party of submachine-gun-toting security staff and bundled into a transit van with blacked out windows. Admittedly we did look suspect, with our crudely, Bic shaven boneheads. The 'haircut' was the handiwork of Frankie, a deranged Glaswegian, employed as a dogsbody at the tavérna and who found a disturbing pleasure in hacking off our locks with blunt scissors and planing our skulls with a rusty razor. The penultimate day in Greece saw us wandering around Athens in excruciating pain with bloody wounds all over our craniums. In bright sunshine and with impaired vision – a product of our colossal hangovers, we studied our 'Bring out your Dead' appearance in the window of the Mount Olympus Hotel. The handful of brain cells that heroically survived the previous night's ouzo attack returned a unanimous verdict: inviting Frankie to give us a follicle makeover after he had consumed two bottles of Greek brandy, was not necessarily one of Ronan's most inspired plans.

Liz decided that it would be prudent to keep her own ticket, *just in case* she was running late. A bit worrying. I had missed more 'take offs' than I care to remember. Several flights had escaped me by simply overdoing it in the airport bar. If I got into company, or worse still, an impromptu game of poker, the *Bing-Bong* last call announcement would as likely as not fail to alert me to the imminent departure of my aircraft.

I was on my best behaviour today. No alcoholic distractions. Cappuccino Grande (£2.70), a cigarette and the Irish Post, which I ploughed through purposefully for five minutes – without reading a single word. Too busy gawping at the continuous stream of headless chickens; parading to and fro in their day-glo holiday outfits, delirious at the prospect of a temporary respite from December's inclement weather and the impending, Christmas credit card overload. Finally I settled on the Malcolm Rogers' page and tried to tune-in on an item about Phil Lynott.

I love you from the bottom of my cappuccino cup. I abandoned the article halfway through and put the Irish Post in my carrier bag: 12.5 grams of Golden Virginia, a Danish pastry and two more cappuccinos' minus the cocoa powder later, and Liz had still failed to appear at the designated meeting place. She had 45 minutes to show. I was going to fly regardless. If she stood me up, I'd be more than a trifle disappointed, but things were looking up. Tom Paulin, the sagacious poet, critic and all-round gifted Irishman asked if the vacant chair at my table was free. Big mistake, Tom. Before he had time to remove his coat and lay down his leather satchel, I was on his case.

'Love the *Late Review*, Tom. It's my favourite show on the telly. The way you stand your ground; even when Germaine Greer, Tony Parsons and that smug-looking fat bloke with the Kojak try to shout you down. Superb.'

'Thank you. I just say what I believe,' he said with those relaxed, sweet-sounding vocal cords.

'I've got to take you to task on Jackson Pollock, though,' his warm smile cooled somewhat when I launched into a savage attack on the troubled American's nursery art.

'It's a load of fuckin' paint scribble. Talk about the Emperor's new clothes. How did he get away with it?' Tom smiled.

'You're not alone with that interpretation of his work,' too fucking right I'm not, Tom.

'Oh, sorry. Derry Sheehan,' I presented my hand. 'Can I get you a coffee?'

Twenty stimulating minutes were filled discussing 'Northern Ireland' and the Arts with the highbrow legend. He told me that he was fetched to the BBC studios at Shepherd's Bush, where the *Late Review* was recorded live, and then returned to his Oxford home by a Beeb car and driver. Nice job. I could do that. Money for nothing and your chicks for free. That is, of course, if you regard Germaine Greer as being a *chick*.

Time is of the essence, is a legal term. When applied to flying, it meant, get on the big iron bird *now* – or, go home and prepare for a weekend listening to the strained sounds of the *Direct from Dungannon Outlaw*, Padraig Fallon. No offence,

Padraig, but life's too short, son.

Well, as predicted, any lingering drips of stress had all but evaporated. Friday afternoon, 14.55; I'm secure in my seat on my plane. Liz was not going to be my companion as planned. No problem. I didn't even bother to examine the possible reasons for her absence. Belfast was fine by me. Coalisland, and Co. Tyrone, was but a 40-minute cruise along the M1 away. Instead of the Dive Bar in Donegal, I would down sticks in John Devlin's, where the barcounter was so high, you could rest your chin on it. And the Guinness... *So* smooth, *So* sweet: 'Like drinkin' a cup o' tea, boy. It's *too* good, Derry,' my uncle Barney would tell me.

Too good for Barney, certainly. His body might have been ravaged and crippled by the damaging side effects of booze, but, he remained the greatest storyteller in town: *Deadly craic.* With a screwed up face like an old prune, his painstakingly slow, let's go twice around the block before relinquishing the sardonic punchline wit, would attract everyone, young and old, to his throne.

Just as I was warming to the unexpected diversion that Liz's truancy would cause, and seconds before the hatches were battened down, there was change.

'Derry,' Liz waved to me whilst simultaneously apologising to all the cabin crew and scrambling about the floor to gather the contents spilled from her handbag.

Saved by the bell. At the same time as a rather large Yank woman asked my permission to squash her mighty arse next to me, Liz came crashing down the aisle, ricochetting off every other headrest.

'Sorry; excuse me; sorry,' she made it to the back of the plane.'C'mere till I tell ye, Derry. You would not *believe* the hassles gettin' here.'

'Best to sit down and tell me, Liz,' she put a bag in the overhead storage and half the luggage fell on top of her.

'I thought you'd blown me out,' I said.

'No way. Don't be soft, man. Had lunch. Brilliant craic. Some tricky fella only tries to thieve my handbag. Yeh know, my ticket, everything was in there, Derry. My worst nightmare. Brona's boyfriend, George, caught the frigger rooting through it in the boys' toilet.'

'How was your friend?'

'Ah, she's grand. Marrying George next summer. She's settlin' down. Loves London.'

'Strange lady.'

'Actually, she's *very* strange. *They go joggin' every night in matching tracksuits!'* she whispered.

'That's not strange; it's downright perverted.'

WELCOME TO BELFAST: like the players who touch the *THIS IS ANFIELD* plaque at Liverpool before they trot out onto the pitch, on tiptoes, I reached out to the dangling sign as I passed under.

'How long's the drive to Donegal, Liz?'

'Get your boot down and we'll make it for six.'

'No sweat.'

Just as I like it. Deep, purple-blue skies: torrential rain was beating down on the roof of our Toyota Corolla and followed us all the way to Donegal. The fresh, manure-smelling air that we both craved wafted in through the open vents. Liz handed me a ham and tom sarnie, kindly made by Noeleen, who was worried that we might forget to eat for two days. Liz fiddled with the dial on the radio and found Ballyshannon Country and, as darkness fell, Glen Campbell provided the perfect early-evening soundtrack with a stirring, melancholic interpretation of the 'Wichita Lineman'. For a brief passage of time (half a kilometre), I *was* the Wichita Lineman: *searching for another overload*. A wave of spray from the truck in front soaked our windscreen and snapped me out of character.

RATHMULLAN 2km.

'We're home and dry, Derry; well... home but,' Liz corrected herself.

'Is your mum alright about me staying?'

'She was a bit shaken when I told her I'd have a man in tow.'

'I bet. Not used to you bringin' mysterious fellas from England home, then?'

'Hardly. I said for her not to wait up. I still have my own key.'

'She will, though, of course.'

'Naturally. Tea, cakes and soda bread will be laid out on the table waitin' for us.'

'Cool. Lookin' forward to meeting her. Is home far from town?'

'No, we're only a ten-minute drive. It's an ol' bungalow off a winding ol' road. Nearest neighbour's half a mile away. Dad has the back yard full up with turf. And when I say full, Derry, I mean *full*. He must have an articulated lorry-load of the stuff carved up.'

'He likes a fire?'

'He likes a fire, is right. You'll get yer face burnt off sittin' in his parlour. He's up out of his seat messin' with the poker every two seconds. You need a feckin' skin graft by the time you get out. Drives Ma nuts, so he does.'

'Nice, though; the old fires.'

'They're wonderful.

Very dirty but. Everyone around here's changing over to the oil. The boys delivering the coal will be lucky to sell a couple of bags a week before long.'

'Sign of the times, Liz.'

'It's not all doom and gloom. There's things starting to happen in Ireland. Bricks are being laid on every spare blade of grass. Builders are actually coming home from London to work. God knows who's buyin' 'em up, but they're selling.'

'Surprised me, the prices they were lookin' in Dublin. Two months ago I was over, 130K for a three-bed in Walkinstown. Unreal.'

'You have business in Dublin, Derry. London to Dublin's the busiest air-route in Europe. It's nearly double the traffic goin' between London and Paris,' said Liz proudly.

'I bet there's not a lot of people who know that.'

'No need to take the piss, Derry. I was just sayin'.'

'Sorry. The seeds are set. The brain drain's in reverse.'

'Something like that. Are we not back, Derry!?'

****

The town square was alive with under twenties. Cars double parked by all the shops and pubs. No such thing as road etiquette here. The Chinese takeaway next to the Dive Bar had a flock of youths feasting on curry-chips. Time: 17.57.

'Nice work, Derry. Look, they've even stopped the rain for us!'

Richard Of York Gave Battle In Vain. A glorious rainbow was projected across a brightening blue sky. Clouds no more. And then it went dark. It went so dark, that I fell on the stairs leading down to the Dive Bar. I took Liz with me as well. We both crashed through the swing door and landed in a mess of 'cartoon fight' arms and legs, sprawled out on the linoleum floor, like a couple of skittles demolished by a bullet-paced bowling ball.

Kajagoogoo, with 'Too Shy' were resounding out from the make shift sound-system set up on a small stage area. Spread-eagled on the deck, I checked out the clientèle with some rapid eye movement. The place was empty (thank you, sweet Jesus) except for a James Joyce doppelgänger, complete with a trilby and round specs, seated at the bar. The music was loud but, even so, he would of heard the racket we had made. He didn't look up from his pint. However, out of my vision, and directly behind us, was the table at which Liz and her close-knit circle of friends had taken up residence on umpteen Fridays past. And, yes, compressed around the table was ten, maybe twelve, Rose of Tralee-class ladies. Four or five of them had their glass suspended in mid-air, frozen, stunned by the spectacle which occupied their space.

I look up at the digital clock above the door: 18.00 flashes. Liz and I rise.

'Six o'clock, the Dive Bar, Rathmullan, Donegal. Did I not promise you a miracle?'

'You did,' Liz initiated our second ever kiss. 'About time I introduced you, Derry.'

Liz acted as usher, holding my hand, sheepishly, I followed a step behind.

'O'Grady, you old bitch, yeh!' Hugs and kisses.

'That's our Anna Livia,' said Liz.

'Sisters?' I asked.

'Her favourite cous,' said Anna.

'Curse enough to live with,' qualified Liz.

'Why didn't you phone us, cous. I'd have come and lifted you from the airport; and *who* is this stranger?'

'This, is Derry.'

'Charmed, I'm sure,' Anna turned away. 'He's gorgeous,

Liz,' she hissed into Liz's ear.

'Derry, say hello to Maeve and Dolores,' two further members of Liz's gang sidled up close to me.

'God, you're a sly one. I nearly died when I realised it was you fallin' in through the door, Liz. It's great to have you home, darlin',' said a deliriously happy Dolores embracing Liz.

'Any craic, Derry?' asked Maeve. 'Do you always make such explosive entrances?'

'Don't like to be ignored, Maeve. I seek attention!'

'You got that, with some style, now. You'll have the key to Rathmullan tonight, Derry,' said Maeve.

'You couldn't please Liz, Derry. She'd need a man with 3 balls; even then, she wouldn't be happy. You've picked the wrong girl there, boy.'

'Frig off, Dolores. You'll have Derry runnin' out on me,' said Liz not looking desperately concerned at the prospect.

'My heart is low, my heart is so low. As only a woman's heart can know.' Difficult to believe, but all conversation ceased, and I was regaled by a remarkably in-tune chorus of the epic Eleanor McEvoy ballad.

Less than one hour of our 'big night' out had expired, and loose lips were already sinking ships. The craicometer was soaring towards 89, which considering that we hadn't yet reached 7pm, the oddly set high of 90, was going to be hit far too soon.

'VIDEO KILLED THE RADIO STAR,' was chanted by one and all (apart from the Joyce clone).

'I don't believe this, Liz: Kajagoogoo and Buggles – on the same night!'

Soaked in sweat, from the intoxicating mix of 'feel good' tunes from the much maligned '80s and, the sweet rhythm of the Donegal dialect, the climate was about to intensify. Just when it looked safe to leave the swaying throng to buy an overdue round, the undisputed, all-time No.1 disco floor-filler, Jocelyn Brown's 'Somebody Else's Guy', sent Liz's party loco. Table tops were mounted: the screeching, gyrating lithe figures of Liz and her posse, had the 'on the pull' men in the, by now, filled Dive Bar, hiding bulges and putting fingers to their lips to wipe dribble.

I was hoisted up onto a small, rickety round table by Dolores and Anna, which was probably not designed to hold six pissed dancing queens. The microphone (an empty bottle of Harp) was thrust to my mouth.

'C'mon, Derry: you are the one, that makes me feel, *so real*. SING!' demanded Anna.

Being the only man in the party, and receiving an outrageous outpouring of tactile attention from a bevy of sparkling, prime local talent, would be a good reason for the regular predators in the Dive Bar to eye me with evil intent. A newcomer with a London accent could only inflame malevolent jealousy. I was, therefore, barely audible when ordering the beer.

Lisa McFadden accompanied Liz when she moved to England. It was too much of a culture shock for Lisa. She left as soon as her savings went. Four weeks after a tearful double send-off hooley at the Dive Bar, she was back on the line in the chicken factory.

Lisa pushed through the two-deep crowd at the bar and ousted the bloke to my right. Ten anxious minutes I spent, whistling nothing, waiting to get served before success: with tits pushed up to her chin, it took Lisa one second to capture the barman's notice.

'I'll give you a hand, Derry. I wanna take a wee nip of

vodka with my Harp – here, take the difference,' I shunned her money.

'Go 'way, Lisa,' she thanked me with a firm handshake.

'Friday's deadly in here, Derry. What d'yeh think of it – are you enjoying yourself?'

'Love it here. I don't want to leave on Sunday. Liz definitely won't.'

'Don't you believe it. As long as you get on that plane, she'll be sittin' next to you.'

'I wouldn't be too sure about that.'

'Are ya jokin' me? I've never seen her like this in my life, the girl hasn't shut up from singing your praises.'

'Serious?'

'Fuck, I'm serious, Derry.'

'We have a future, then?' Lisa's opinion, I decided, carried weight.

'What's the deal with youse two? I had a letter off Liz about a week ago. She never even mentioned you – *or*, that she was coming home.'

'Well, *we* didn't exist when she wrote the letter.'

'I love it. Your eyes meet across a crowded room – there's a slight parting of lips – you exchange a *you're the one for me* smile, and rush into each others arms: two become one,' Lisa's eyes closed gently, as she drew clenched fists to her heart.

'*Oh yeah*, that exactly.'

'Twenty-three twelve,' said the barman with a hand stretched vaguely in my direction, and with his head pursuing Lisa's Grand Canyon of a cleavage.

I followed in Lisa's slipstream and a sea of bodies parted as a path to our table was forged. She twisted her head back and yelled in my ear: 'I couldn't live there, Derry.'

'London?' The Waterboys made it hard for me to hear Lisa.

The music was much louder than when we arrived.

'Everything passed me by, Derry. My head was spinnin' after a week. I don't know how you can stand it.'

'It's not that bad. You didn't give yourself time to adjust.'

'Too fast. The whole place is too fast: cars, people – work work work, *sleep*, then it's time to go to work, again!'

'What's that blade bitchin' about now, Derry? She missed her mammy's cookin', is all,' said Liz trawling the empties to create some space.

Liz pulled me into a clinch: *'Thunder only happens when it's raining,'* she crooned. 'I love this song, Derry*.' There was a long pause before Liz continued. 'I love you, Derry.' I waited for a laugh, but there wasn't one. She was serious. Serious drink talk, at any rate.

'Why didn't you go out with me when I asked you six months ago, then?' I asked innocently.

'Get real! I get a dozen offers every night in the pub. It's a joke. The more pints they have, the more desirable I get. How could I go out with someone in the Crown?'

'Time moves on, though; and here we are.'

'It was so nice of you to set this little break up, Derry. I really needed a fix. Lisa was right. It's tough being away.'

'There's no law sayin' that you have to go back to Seven Kings. Is there?'

'You know why I left in the first place, Derry. You want to prove things to yourself. You have to do it.'

Copious pints of Guinness were hoovered up, when to my veiled relief, the staff, at last gathered in the bar towels. Only three sponges were left dealing with the dregs of their pints. It was 2.30. I staggered up the stairs to the street. Liz pro-

* 'Dreams' Fleetwood Mac

ceeded to spend the best part of the next hour saying goodbye to her friends.

Night had not yet turned to day when Liz bundled me into a cab, but the dawn chorus, and sun-up would face my fragile shell approximately six hours before I was willing.

'You alright, boy?' asked Liz concerned by my new colour.

'Wrecked, Liz.'

'Strong stout here, Derry. I did warn yeh.'

'I'm not complainin'. It was a great night.'

* * * * * * *

The rest of Ireland was 'up and at it' long before my eyelids were compliant and able to work in an opening movement. Attempting to keep my jelly brain as still as possible, I made a stab at stirring my torpid members into action, and fell off the bed. Ever since Liz's sister, Fallon, migrated to Clones, this was the spare room.

I crawled over the floor to the window and gripped the curtains with both hands. I rejoiced in the strength of my arms. Very impressively, I thought, they hauled me up to the window ledge. I forced the curtains, tugging them open before noticing the cords provided. Not only was there sunshine, but beyond the 'turf mountain', was land. No office blocks; no high-rise flats; no shops and, more significantly, no people.

A lone cow was munching grass in a field of her own. The only job she had today was lumbering around eating grass. My job was far more taxing: I had to try and make myself look presentable for Liz *and* to her parents – keep down a fry, and consume more Guinness. Can I be a cow, please? I asked my cadaverous reflection.

Frantically, I flattened my ear up against the door and

counted the number of voices flowing in the kitchen. Nightmare. Four at least – no, five... six, they're having a bloody family reunion. My watch stopped at half-past eleven the night before. I didn't have a clue what the time was. There was no sink to douse my face and correct my hair. The only route to the bathroom was to walk through the kitchen. Thanks, Liz, I cursed her selfishly.

A bit of spit sorted out the hair problem. Although not possessing the density or 'shape and hold' value of gel, it worked to shore up the fringe in an emergency. I truly did not want to meet the O'Grady family without cleaning my teeth. Lonely are the brave, as they say. In slow motion, I pushed down on the handle, fully aware that even the slightest noise and turn of the handle on the other side, would alert and, divert, the attention of the 'kitchen dwellers' to the bedroom door.

'My God! It's the Return of the Living Dead!' announced Liz.

Liz's mum greeted me with an invigorating smile which relaxed me at once. She was slim and beautiful. I couldn't help but blurt out: 'Your skin's as smooth as a baby's bum. You have green eyes; you're gorgeous!' Did I just say that? I did, and it went down very well. The kitchen was congested, my head count was five light. The smell emanating from the frying-pan was actually well received by my aching belly. Angela, Liz's ma, introduced her three sisters, Pauline, Theresa and Slany.

'Ladies, I must apologise. What with the jet-lag and the booze, I look a right mess. But I'm really pleased to meet you all. Liz talks about you all the time when she's over in England.'

'Sit down, Derry. You look fine to me, son,' said Pauline. 'Breakfast's ready.'

'Thank you. What time is it, Liz?'

'Nine.'

'*Nine*? It can't be. Can I go back to bed?' I pleaded.

Slany, the youngest of Liz's aunties – and, the one I had been warned of, was looking me up and down like Devout Donnagán, the deeply religious, psychotic bouncer who used to vet the punters and patrol the dance floor at the Room At The Top nightclub in Ilford. He lost his job when the owners found out that he would only grant entry to the 'clubbers' if they could successfully recite a passage from the Bible.

We had not made direct eye contact, but she made me feel self-conscious and, temporarily, shy. I was waiting for her to come over and check the back of my ears and neck for evidence of poor cleanliness. The fact that Slany was the 'baby' out of the four girls, did not prevent her from being the boss. Slany called a spade a spade and, at one time or another, had upset all her sisters, with her cutting and forthright opinions. She wasted no time in ripping into me.

'So you're the reason Liz hasn't been to visit, or even bother to phone me, then?' With half a sausage and plump mushroom speared on my fork, I took a proper look at Slany. *You don't scare me, lady*. I dipped into a pool of brown sauce.

'Your parents are Irish?'

'Tyrone... And Longford.'

'What job is it you do?' the grilling continued.

'Building work. Renovating flats and houses for a property developer.'

'That's good wages in London, is it, Derry?' asked Pauline.

'Can be, Pauline. Work drys up, though. It's an expensive city to live in when that happens.'

'I know, Derry. I have a sister living at Wembley. Tom, her husband, he drives a truck. They pay the mortgage, the bills.

What's left?'

'Peanuts. You struggle on, Pauline.'

'You should come and live in Ireland, Derry. A bright lad like you would have no problem here,' said Angela.

'You need to be Irish to settle in Ireland. Everyone loves it here when they come over on holiday. When you're living here, it's completely different,' said Slany sharpening her claws.

'I am *Irish*. I was born in Coalisland. County Tyrone,' I said to Slany in particular.

'See that, Slany,' said Angela patting me on the back. 'The boy's pure.'

'Coalisland; that's a 'hot spot'. That place is always on the news. We have a Rebel in our midst,' decided Slany.

'I don't go round preaching politics. All I believe in, is equality.'

'See!' said Slany. 'Did I not tell yeh so. *He's a Rebel!*' this remark did at least convey the genesis of a smile from Slany.

'Leave the boy alone,' said Theresa. 'Finish up your breakfast, Derry.'

* * * * * * *

We went for a long walk after breakfast. Liz pointed out St. Mhuire's, her old primary school, and a host of other symbolic landmarks which held cherished memories from a blessed childhood.

'You know what really pisses me off?' I declared.

'The rain?' The pleasant, cold-warmth of early morning was now replaced by intermittent storms which left us wet and, in my case, soaked.

'No. You can't argue with the rain. It has a function.'

'What, then, the way us girls split open the crisp bag and lay it flat on the table?'

'Yeah, that *does* piss me off, Liz, but it wasn't what I was thinking of; that's No.2 on the list.'

'Number one?'

'Time: all these trees, acres of unspoilt land – the mountains. They're just goin' to go on and on.'

'Without us,' Liz gazed wistfully at the lavish, sodden panorama.

'Without you and I, my dear, is correct. I want to tread every inch of this country. I've wasted so many days, Liz.'

'We could live forever, Derry.'

'*We can*, if we try.'

7. BECAUSE THE NIGHT

As sure as night follows day, and as certain as Jimmy Greaves' league and international goals-per-game ratio will be impossible to equal or better, Liz remained in Ireland. I knew she would.

The reason for the vacant seat on the return flight, and the deserted feeling it left me with – compared to the euphoric promise of the outgoing journey – was, however, not the one I anticipated. Her big sis gave birth to a weak, jaundice-tanned six-pounder, baby Sonia. Fallon was delirious with joy, the emergency Caesarean section which provoked the surgeon's messy scalpel assault on her tummy, and the subsequent agony and discomfort it inflicted, was soon dispelled, if not forgotten. Inconvenient though it was for the short-term development of our relationship – but, perfectly natural under the circumstances, Liz was hastily despatched to Clones by Angela, to give some family support to Fallon.

Whilst not harbouring any bitterness or ill-feeling toward the tot, her five-weeks' premature coming, was bad fucking timing: *I didn't mean that, Lord.* I promised him that I would send a cute and cuddly 'something' special delivery.

The Saturday night was a low-key affair, spent with Angela and Peter, Liz's dad, in a cramped bar which was attached to a community hall, locally known as the Boxing Club. There was still a ring set up in the hall, and this was a legendary ring, made so by the Rathmullan Gladiator, the exalted Willie Doolan who won 'bronze' in the featherweight division at the Mexico Olympics.

Peter was a decent, hard-working man and, to my great relief, *we bonded* – due in no small part to our shared passion for Gaelic football and horse-racing. A splendid evening was not ruined by the barman (Peter's brother) refusing to take any money from me.

Back down to earth and the realities of life with a rocklike thump on the head. Cliff informed me of Eamon's instruction: a call on the home of Colin McLynn was a Monday morning priority. Colin weathered a massive heart attack on Friday morning, surviving only long enough for a second, less potent strike to terminate his gallant resistance later that afternoon.

'Make a visit to the house, Cliff,' he said. 'The daughter, Sarah-Jane, will be there sorting through his old junk. She works in a bank – high up, mind – she'll understand it's only business. I hope. Poor Colin still owes me six-hundred quid.'

'She won't know anything about a loan "arrangement" with Eamon if she works in a bank,' I told Cliff. 'Colin would of been too proud to tell her that he couldn't make ends meet.'

Colin had made his contribution to society. A thirty-year stint of back-snapping *shovel and pickin'* for O'Keeffe's on North London's 'granite' roads claimed another Irishman's scalp. The hands were ravaged by arthritis, his once iron grip like a child's.

As if I was not already acutely aware of the partially selfish grounds for our Donegal trip, ie – escaping from the prosaic rut I was in for a few days (and, in doing so, giving Liz's battery a charge), it crystallised a fermenting belief that I was blithe to embrace. Turning my back on family and friends would be a wrench, and on occasion, fill me with guilt and regret. But working for Eamon was not my idea of fun and gave me zero job-satisfaction, not to mention dilution of a sagging self-esteem. Moving back to Ireland was very much on the cards.

Raising a 'proper' wedge to go with was the first, and only practical step to address. Decisions were easy to make, seeing them through to the desired end, was my problem. Not this time, though. Apathy is the most contemptible word in the dictionary, it reeks. Because of a lack of ambition and direction, I had dug a deep hole in Seven Kings, and if I didn't climb out of it now, I probably never would.

* * * * * * *

Ciaran White called me and had some diamond-clustered news to impart. The Ostrich, the nag which we both had a grand riding on, romped home by three lengths, thus setting the ball rolling on the funds 'issue' with a whopping £12,000. The second phone-call I received on Monday morning, however, from Liz, was the life-giving tonic required to face up to the day's duties. Things were progressing nicely in Clones, with Sonia's growing strength exceeding the doctor's cautious forecast. Liz would be back soon.

Cliff binged the weekend, cramming 7 days into 2, and his usual in-ya-face, speeding tongue was subdued by the wanton swallowing of double-shot Bacardi, following on from a dozen pints of stout. I left him alone as we cruised round town. Normally I would seize the opportunity and penetrate his weakened defence, showing no mercy with the slagging. Our affable dialogue was refreshingly grown-up, if somewhat disjointed and monotone.

Although the drink put the brakes on, Cliff was born with a remarkably-resilient constitution, and was still able to rise early on Sunday morning to keep the established swimming date with Luke, arriving at our house bang on eight. There was no question that if he'd been born in (World) wartime, the trenches would have been inspirited by his attendance. He was indestructible in many ways.

'I was thinkin' I might go to South Africa, Derry.'

'You've already been on that excursion, mate. That place is like Saigon 30 years ago. They're all jumpin' fuckin' ship and coming over here,' I advised him.

'I was on the phone to Carl last night. Off me fuckin' brain, rambling on for hours. Mum's gonna kill me when the bill turns up. Carl promised me work.'

'You're a qualified tractor driver, Cliff. The world's your backyard.'

'This job's bollocks, Derry. You know it.'

'It might do you a turn for the rest of winter: Swanning about his mum's ranch, relaxing by the pool, with their slave bringin' you drinks out on a silver tray.'

'Carl doesn't have slaves. They're staff. They have a better life, a proper education for their kids.'

'Don't talk shit, Cliff. They're slaves. Better dressed, a few more rands in their pockets. *Slaves*. Besides, Carl's like all the other Afrikaner's that I've ever met. Extremely boring.'

'I'm not going to argue. You're in one of those moods,' said Cliff turning away.

'Tell you the truth, I was thinking of chuckin' it in and re-locating, as well,' I confessed.

'Ireland?'

'It's under consideration.'

'You're all talk, Derry.' Cliff answered his mobile.

'Yes, boss. No, boss. *Mayfair!* Right... right, yeah, right. No problem. D'yeh want Derry?' Cliff passed the phone. 'Mr Mooney would like to talk.'

'Hi'ya, Eamon. Yes, Eamon. No, Eamon. *The Park Lane*

Hotel! Who is 'e?'

A distinguished visitor, Pascal Toye, the Canadian Ambassador to Ireland, was in London. Camden Council were according him a Civic Reception, hosted by the Council Chairman, Mr. Colm Ceann who happened to be a close pal of Eamon's.

Eamon was having kittens. 'Get ya motor cleaned – shave ya feckin' face – buy some of them smelly Christmas tree dangles. And tell Cliff *not* to speak! Oh, by the way, he's pissed, and has wandered into the red-lights of Shepherd Market, gone with a tart and hasn't any cash to pay her with. The wife's goin' bananas, pullin' out her hair in the hotel waitin' for him with the kids. She was convinced that terrorists had kidnapped the silly ol' fucker. I've managed to calm her down – said that he's bumped into the Duke of Beckton, and he invited him back to his castle for tea and crumpet – you've got one hour to rescue him, sober him up and get him back to the hotel. Did yeh have a nice wee holiday!?'

'Do what! Have you been on the poteen, Eamon?'

The Ambassador was to give a keynote speech in the hallowed chambers of Camden Council. The theme of his oration was the Irish rovers who had shifted to Canada – and the profound effect that their addition had made on North American Culture, and how their productive input of labour helped boost the Economy – at 3pm.

'There used to be a great little Turkish restaurant in Shepherd Market – just round the corner from the Grapes pub,' remembered Cliff.

'Can you just forget eating? You have as much chance of calling in there for a shish kofte as Mr Toye has of giving an erudite address, today.'

'He's probably dead by now. Stabbed by the ripper's pimp.

Does Eamon want us to baby-sit him all day?'

'Yeah,' I said. 'All day, and all bloody night.'

'This Pascal character, he could be a useful contact for Canada. What d'yeh think? A bit of a delicate situation we're dealing with here, what with the poor wife and kids just round the corner. Big scandal if this one slipped out, mate.' Cliff's evil mind was becoming increasingly fertile.

'South Africa's out now, is it?'

'I fancy meself in that climate, Derry. It's the land of opportunity – and SEX! The place where real men and real women have insatiable appetites. All that snow; you spend a lot of long, long nights holed up in them log cabins, boy,' Cliff sprouted the befitting Leslie Phillips' smirk.

****

'You guys really saved my bacon here, today – and Pascal Toye is not a man who forgets a good Samaritan. No, Sir.'

'It was our privilege to be of service, Ambassador,' grovelled Cliff courting favour.

'Hell, call me Pascal, Clifford, we're not on ceremony here, son. I guess you fellas put old Pascal up on a pedestal,' the Ambassador reduced his voice to a whisper as we shivered into a huddle on the corner of Down Street. 'Underneath this powerful Diplomatic cloak that I wear with pride beats the heart of a regular, living and breathing, humble man – pulsing the blood of our two great nations.' I wiped a tear. Not so much Pascal's emotive words as the arctic bite of the wind.

I thought better of asking Pascal what he actually received for the 300 notes it cost me to extricate him from Madame Charlene's 'classy' boudoir. Eamon would pay. I was preoccupied with the next stage of the job: operation Bullshit Wife.

I need not of worried. Mrs Toye was dancing with the same fairies as Pascal.

'The Duke of Beckton! My God! Why didn't you get a photograph, Pascal? Are they directly related to the Queen, Derry?' she gasped dropping her unlit cheroot.

'I believe he is,' I said enthusiastically. 'Not quite sure of the exact line, though, Tammy.'

The mini-bar in the bedroom-suite had taken a severe caning. Plenty of mixers left. Cliff had a bitter lemon, I had a dry ginger ale as we watched the children play 'trampolines' on the king-size bed and Tammy turned to see how big her bum looked in the full-length mirror. Her eggy-yellow, Hillary Clinton power-suit was not a great fit and made her look fatter than she was.

'Stunning,' said Cliff. 'Ab-solute-ly stunning, Tammy.' She tiptoed over in spike stilettos and pinched both of Cliff's cheeks: '*You* are such a gentleman, Clifford (he displayed a cute blush). Did you hear that, Pascal? Clifford says Tammy looks *stunning!*'

'Damned straight you do, Baby-Doll.' Pascal sent me the 'got out of jail free' wink.

It could of been a fry-up the way he wiped around the plate with his roll. As a matter of fact, it was Roast Salmon with Mozzarella, and Squid Ink Risotto.

Pascal insisted that we join him for lunch in Bracewell's Restaurant, positioned off the middle of the hotel's tea lounge, where a harp was gently, and lovingly plucked by an unsmiling lady who wore her theatrical gown and age with old-fashioned dignity.

'We'd best get rolling, Pascal,' I prompted. 'There's a hall, full of people eager to hear you speak, sir.'

'Slow down, Derry,' said Pascal. 'There is *always* time for cherry cheesecake.' Cliff nodded vigorously in agreement.

Pascal performed brilliantly. When you put him on a platform, he was devastating. My cynical view of him changed very quickly. In cinematic terms, it was up there with the greatest moment in Hollywood history, the last Russian roulette scene from *The Deer Hunter*, when Christopher Walken fleetingly, at last recognises Robert De Niro before clicking the cylinder round to a full chamber: 'One shot.'

Cliff got busy networking the dignitaries, presenting himself as a Bruce Willis-style bodyguard for the rich and influential. Each time an arm appeared through the crowd holding aloft a tray of drinks, Cliff lifted a flute of Dom Perignon. I was keeping a close eye on Pascal. He was on his best behaviour. The Ambassador and Tammy were working as a double-act tonight. Colm Ceann was delighted with the way that the official proceedings had gone.

'Derry, is it?' asked Ceann.

'Yes, Mr Ceann.'

'You're one of Eamon's men?'

'Yes, sir.'

'I appreciate the discreet and professional way you handled the earlier complications. I didn't find it one bit funny, Derry. I shall be giving Eamon a glowing reference; you and your partner's efforts will not be forgotten by me,' Colm tapped his nose to emphasise the point.

'That's no problem, Mr Ceann.'

Cliff barged in shaking his phone in the air.

'What you playin' at you silly minge?' I screamed.

'What's a matter with you?' said Cliff guiltless.

'This is work you prick, not an end of season jolly-up.'

'I'm mixing business with expensive, *free* champagne. Lighten up, Derry. I've got your mum on the phone.'

'MUM! *Slow down*. What *exactly* did she say?'

'Her sister's wee ba has been rushed into intensive care. It's serious, Derry; she was crying, *and crying*. Get in touch with her son.'

****

I didn't bother to telephone the hospital. The last flight to Dublin out of London City Airport was 21.10. I had abandoned the Ambassador, leaving him in Cliff's dubious care. I screeched to a halt, bang outside the main entrance, parking on double-yellow lines, and inviting my car's removal.

I made the Aer Lingus desk at 20.51. They allowed me to join the businessmen on flight RE238. So grateful to American Express was I, when the £60 one-way ticket was authorised on my over-the-limit account, I reached over to name-badge wearing Heli and grazed her cheek with a kiss before grabbing my ticket.

I bombed up the escalator to Departures. Then, I slid straight back down the 40ft rubber handrail on the escalator and landed in the lap of a customer sat at *Steve's Shoe Shine* booth. Apologising to Steve and client, I ran across to check-in and snatched my boarding card off the startled, but helpful Sandy: 'Sorry, thank you,' I shouted flying back up the escalator.

I boarded at 21.09. *Easy*. My heart was thumping against my skin like a jack hammer.

****

St. Darley's General Hospital, Clones: six minutes to one.

'*Wake up it's a beautiful morning*,' the Boo Radleys could be heard on a distant radio from a staff room at the end of a corridor. The wards were silent. A cleaning man was buffing a high-gloss on the terracotta-coloured floor by reception.

Liz walked slowly down the corridor, stopping at the drinks machine. She didn't notice me. A plastic cup dropped down and filled with coffee. Liz began walking even more slowly to where I was standing. She was still unaware of my presence. I didn't want to speak. Her face was drained of colour. Tears gathered on her eyelashes. Liz looked up and saw me standing motionless. My eyes filled up. We sat down.

'She had meningitis. Sonia's dead. We've lost her, Derry.' I couldn't speak. I had rehearsed a few empty words of comfort on the plane, but I couldn't speak.

'Don't ever leave me, Derry. Don't *ever* fucking leave me.'

'I love you, Liz. I couldn't leave you if I tried.' We were both crying.

'It doesn't feel very Christmassy. Does it, Derry?'

an deireadh

[illegible] to sit down and [illegible],' she put a bag in the overhead storage and [illegible] on top of her.

'I thought you [illegible].'

'No [illegible]. Don't be [illegible]. [illegible] brilliant craic. [illegible] only [illegible] my handbag [illegible] everything [illegible] Dunn! My worst nightmare. [illegible]'s boyfriend [illegible] caught the trigger rooting through it in the boys' toilet.'

'How was your friend?'

'Oh, she's grand. Marrying [illegible] next summer. She's settled [illegible]. Loves London.'

'[illegible] strange lady.'

'[illegible], she's *very strange*. [illegible] *go jogging every night in* [illegible] *tracksuits!*' she whispered.

'That's not strange, it's [illegible].'

WELCOME TO BELFAST [illegible] the plane [illegible] the *[illegible] FIELD* plaque [illegible] on the pitch, on tiptoes. [illegible] a sign [illegible].

'How long's that [illegible]?'

[illegible]

[illegible]